Whirling Dance
of Planets

A Pocket Manual
for Interpreting
Astrological Transits

ROSANNE FINN

Also by Rosanne Finn ~
The Journey-work of the Stars: An Astrology Workbook

Quote on page iii used with
Permission from the estate of Marion Zimmerman Bradley

DEDICATION

For my spiritual teachers who introduced me to many of the
great books listed: CB (1983-6), Miiller (1987-8), Ze'ev (1988),
Swami Kripalvananda and his disciples (1988-1992), Shaun
(1993-4), Masao (1994-5), Shira (1994-5), and Dan (1998-2001),
all who arrived in my life during my Jupiter Dasha (1985-2001).
Every time I turned away from my spiritual path and decided I
had enough seeking, another brilliant teacher entered my life,
either by reminding me to breathe when I felt the most lost
(Swami K.), offering me a job (Masao), disguised as a lover
(Miiller) or therapist (Ze'ev and Shira) or college professor (CB
and Shaun), or inviting me to write their book (Dan). I thank
you all. Little did I know how precious your teachings would be
to me or how extraordinary it is to have others light the path.

CONTENTS

THE WHIRLING DANCE OF PLANETS

ACKNOWLEDGMENTS

Carol, for editing and being a steady source of support, Marie for keeping me on track and encouraging me whenever I got stuck, Shari for being a wellspring of creative inspiration, my son Finn for being such a thoughtful, kind and respectful teenage boy and breaking all the negative stereotypes of teenage boys that I was taught.

Astrology is the act of decoding the messages of the sky. Since everything is interconnected through a web of energy, we are intrinsically connected to the sky. The sky is a large reflection of our inner make up. In the realm of time and space, there are messages for our purpose of being and direction of greatest happiness. As we fully embrace the sky pattern at our birth, we move into greater wholeness. As the sky changes, as the planets move, we are taught through resonance to accept our fate, to develop our gifts, to follow our calling and to face our challenges. Within the flow of life is peace and happiness.

". . . as I learned again to count sun tides from equinox to solstice and back to equinox again . . . count them painfully on my fingers like a child or a novice priestess; it was years before I could feel them running in my blood again, or know to a hairline's difference where on the horizon moon or sun would rise or set for the salutations I learned again to make. Again, late at night while the household lay sleeping round me, I would study the stars, letting their influence move in my blood as they wheeled and swung around me until I became only a pivot point on the motionless earth, center of the whirling dance around and above me, the spiraling movement of the seasons."

~ from *The Mists of Avalon*
by Marion Zimmer Bradley

Introduction

A **transit** is when a planet in the sky at some point in time makes an aspect, which is an angle, to a planet in the sky at a *different* point in time. Usually we are looking at the placement and movement of the planets at a certain time in connection to a birth chart. Transits are ways of looking at the cycles in which planets move as they orbit the Sun. Transits are the human experience of sacred geometry— the planets dancing in geometric shapes with each other in time and space, exciting an experience of the sacred in one way or another.

A **natal chart** is a snapshot of the planets and stars at the moment that something is born, be it a person, a company, a project, a building, a country, could be anything. In the moment something is born, it breathes in the heavens. It takes in the entire Universe. It is a reflection of all that is occurring at that moment. Since all life, all things, are interconnected at the very core of existence, the birth is the moment that a thing comes into form. That which was non-existent one moment becomes its own unique presence in this world. When we move through the birthing canal, we change form from fetus, being completely held and sustained through our mother, into the form of a person who breathes and exists outside of the womb. This is a magnificent transformation and is marked by all that is occurring in the Universe and beyond. The natal chart displays a part of that moment—it shows the planets, the stars, the Sun, and the Moon among other points that may be used by an astrologer.

Our natal chart is the song we sing throughout life. It is a tone, a harmony, a melody, a resonance, a chord, a picture. It is not stagnant. It is alive. We move with it. We accept it. We resist it. We love it. We hate it. We acknowledge it. We forget it.

Our natal chart is a blueprint, a map of tendencies. The more we become aware of our tendencies, the more our awareness grows, the greater our perspective becomes, the less we resist what is and the more we can change what is changeable. There is no end to the number of perspectives in the world. Any situation, any picture can be observed through infinity of lenses. Problems can look like bliss through another's eyes. Pleasure can look like suffering from one moment to another. Our perspective is not only about actual sight, although that can certainly be part of it. Perspective is about awareness. The more we are aware, the more we are conscious and awake, the greater our perspective becomes and the more choice we have.

When our perspective is so limited that we feel a victim to what has occurred in our life, then our choices are indeed limited. They are limited by what we can perceive and in this space the outcomes are often predictable. When we are open to a greater perspective, then the awareness becomes the healing—and we work with our chart and the transits in order to experience the greatest ease and flow of life. When we feel empowered in life, the choices are endless and there is no way to predict the outcome—we are creating the outcome as we move through time and space.

Understanding our natal chart—and how the Universe is interacting with it at any given moment—is a tool for expanding awareness. It is a tool that helps us to honor our intuition. It supports a greater understanding of life and the parts we play. It is, as far as I can see, not a necessary tool, but a valuable one. In a world that values concrete evidence, astrology is a wonderful tool for our minds. It requires calculation, measurement and repeatability—which it has demonstrated for thousands of years.

When we look at transits, we are looking at how the planets in their orbits are ringing the notes in our natal chart—our home song. We resonate with the frequency, the tone, and the vibration of the transiting planet that is offering us a greater understanding of some aspect of ourselves. The planet transiting is our teacher, our guide for greater awareness. It is showing us the ways we are unconsciousness in connection with the particular point in our chart that is being transited.

By definition, every planet in the sky is transiting every point in our natal chart at all times. What is different is the degree or the extent to which we experience a transit. Some transits are felt more deeply, more concretely. Some transits have a greater "impact" or what feels like an "impact". Some transits have more significant teachings. The extent to which a transit is felt is dependent on the angle (or the harmonic) between the natal and transiting planet, the planets involved, and the speed of the planets in relationship to each other. It is also dependent on our own acceptance and familiarity with the transiting planet as well as the planet being transited. For example, when we have worked through control issues and authority issues related to Saturn, then when Saturn is transited we may experience only a subtle influence. Also, then, transits of Saturn become less problematic and more supportive. If we suffered abuse as a child related to a difficult aspect to the Moon, and we have not emotionally (Moon) dealt with the issue, every transit of the Moon will be felt intensely.

This is the nature of sacred geometry. Each shape holds within it sacred information—sacred content. The shape, formed from angles, has a unique message. Astrology is the act of decoding the sacred geometry of the planets and stars as they move in the sky.

Two Principles of Transits

First: **a slower moving planet** (in relation to Earth—or whatever point of reference is being used) **has a greater influence** since we experience its effect for a longer period of time and have longer to digest and assimilate the teaching.

Second: **the lower the harmonic, the greater the influence**. As in music, the first harmonic rings the loudest. Such as it is with astrology: when two planets are conjunct, meaning they are at the same longitude, the effect is the most intense. (In the next section, I describe harmonics).

Many of us have done a lot of work on ourselves emotionally and spiritually. Therapy and alternative healings are no longer taboo in our culture and more and more are becoming acceptable and normal practices. The transits are becoming less and less predictable for many of us. Yet, it is also helpful to be aware of the subtle influences. Along with healing, we become more sensitive to energies outside the scope of what is detectable through our five senses. The influence of the planets in our lives falls into this category. We cannot hear, see, taste, smell or touch the influence of the planets. Yet, as we become more and more aware of the subtle influences of life—our thought patterns, our emotional states, our energy bodies, our nervous system, our soul yearnings, and on and on—the knowledge of the placement of the planets and their resonating influence on our lives becomes an even more useful and fun tool for living with greater joy and peace.

> *The planet transiting is our teacher, our guide for greater awareness.*

Harmonics

The **harmonic** is simply the number of times the circle (360 degrees) is divided. The first harmonic is no division, an undivided whole. The second harmonic is the wheel divided by two, leaving a 180-degree angle. The third harmonic is the circle divided by three giving a 120-degree angle, and on and on. By the time we get to the ninth harmonic the effect felt is fairly weak, and so most astrologers rarely go beyond the ninth harmonic when looking at transits.

Each harmonic has its own unique style of teaching. The planet is the teacher and represents the content of the lesson. The harmonic tells us how the teaching is presented.

The **1st harmonic** is one of oneness. The two or more planets fuse, merge, and transform into one. Their energies become focused and aligned. They unite and move forward with greater *force*.

Aspects: Conjunction (0°)

The **2nd harmonic** is one of learning through encountering the mirror. We see the opposite. The two planets oppose and bring out the best and worst of each other in a duel that allows us to see the issues of both planets with greatest intensity and light. This is often considered the most difficult of aspects since there is no escape, no way out but *to face the brightness*. The two planets separate and we feel the loss and crisis of the one becoming two.

Aspects: Opposition (180°), Conjunction (0°)

The **3rd harmonic** is one of *strength* and *harmony*. The planets work together to enhance each other. The teachings are presented through a gift that must be uncovered, sought after and acknowledged in order to be received. The teachings come gently and kindly. We must stay open in order to receive them.

Aspects: Trine (120°), Conjunction (0°)

The **4th harmonic** is one of *strife* and *challenge*. We are challenged and forced to work with the lessons of the planets involved. There is no way out but through. The right angle represents the greatest amount of interaction between any two force fields. Thus the fourth harmonic is one of many interactions and much change. This is the harmonic where there is pressure to bring our gifts into form. Thus while the fourth is about *stress* it is also about *manifestation*.

Aspects: Square (90°), Opposition (180°), Conjunction (0°)

The **5ᵗʰ harmonic** is one of *inspiration* and *magic*. It supports learning through creativity. It is a harmonic of altered states of consciousness that are also grounded and even-keeled. It supports us awakening to the lessons of the planets through ritual, artistic expression and divine connection.

Aspects: Quintile (72°), Bi-quintile (144°), Conjunction (0°)

The **6ᵗʰ harmonic** is one of *spiritual connection to the planet Earth*, of grounded *focus* with ease, of *opportunities* and of *love*. In the sixth harmonic we find our greatest connection to nature and animal spirits. We are able to understand and assimilate the teachings of our elders, especially the elders of indigenous cultures. This is a harmonic where the planets' lessons come through connection with others and with real physical possibility.

Aspects: Sextile (60°), Trine (120°), Opposition (180°), Conjunction (0°)

The **7ᵗʰ harmonic** is one of *spiritual connection to the Heavens*, to life forms and existences outside of this planet, Earth. This is the harmonic that is the doorway to the stars. Life is weird and unusual in the seventh harmonic. We encounter lessons through bizarre, and what appear as unnatural, situations. Indeed, this harmonic is unnatural on the physical earth plane and yet it is most natural in the energetic and etheric planes. The seventh harmonic is one that resonates most often with extra-terrestrial activity, unusual events and significant connections with other realms and places. This is also a harmonic which resonates with a message, messenger and with communication. In the seventh harmonic we learn and absorb channeled information, ancient wisdom and spiritual guidance.

Aspects: Septile (51.4°), Bi-septile (102.8°), Tri-septile (154.3°), Conjunction (0°)

The **8th harmonic**, a resonance of the 4th harmonic, is one of *adjustment* and *stress*. We are asked to change, using our will and wisdom. There is a quality of being pushed and edged on to make changes in our lives. The planets teach us through external changes and situations in which we must shift our perspective and attitude in order to live with grace and ease.

Aspects: Semi-square (45°), Sesquiquadrate (135°), Square (90°), Opposition (180°), Conjunction (0°)

The **9th harmonic** is one of *completion* and *clearing*. The three triangles form a figure of great strength and integrity. We are asked through the planets to come to resolution. We must reach a final closure point so that in the next phase we can begin with a clean slate.

Aspects: Novile (40°), Bi-novile (80°), Quart-novile (160°), Trine (120°), Conjunction (0°)

The **10th harmonic**, a resonance of the 2nd and the 5th harmonics, is one of *magic* and *ritual* that must honor both heaven and earth, both the road that leads skyward and the road that is earthbound. The magic of the fifth harmonic is mirrored back to itself and there is no escape. We must create and allow ourselves to be created.

Aspects: Decile (36°), Quintile (72°), Bi-quintile (144°), Tri-decile (108°), Opposition (180°), Conjunction (0°)

The **11th harmonic** is one of *divine inspiration*, a call to study and to meditate. This is a resonance in which those who have mastered life and death are called to reside. In tuning into the eleventh harmonic we find truth and understanding, wisdom and ascension.

Aspects: Un-decile (32.7°) (65.4°) (98.2°) (130.9°) (163.6°), Conjunction (0°)

The **12th harmonic**, a resonance that contains the 2nd, 3rd, 4th, and 6th, is one of *integrity*, truth, and seeing reality as it is. The lessons of this harmonic are contained in needing to accept responsibility and honor our paths and ourselves. The zodiac, based on the twelfth harmonic, contains all stages of life. This is a harmonic of wholeness. This is the harmonic of space, the third dimension and of physical reality including the ability to change physical reality.

Aspects: Semi-sextile (30°), Quincunx (150°), Sextile (60°), Square (90°), Trine (120°), Opposition (180°), Conjunction (0°)

The **13th harmonic** is one of *going beyond limits*. We are challenged, though esoterically, to move past any perceived limitations and concepts. Here in the thirteenth, the planets teach us through showing that life is never what it appears to be. We probably all have associations with the number 13—lucky or unlucky. Thirteen moon cycles in one solar cycle, 13 weeks in a season (13x4=52), 26 earth days for one solar day (13x2), 260 days in a Mayan Sacred Year (13x20), every 13,000 years the Winter Solstice Sun aligns with the Galactic Center and we begin a new round of creation. The Base 12 system used by the Sumerians and in music (12 notes in a chromatic scale) makes the number 13 the octave number or the beginning of the next level. Thirteen is the number of time, the fourth dimension, and our ability to travel through and between realms and altering states of consciousness. Time, while we treat it as a constant, is never constant and as an aspect of speed is only a measure of perception.

Aspects: (27.7°), (55.4°), (83.1°), (110.8°), (138.5°), (166.2°)

Astrology is the act of decoding the sacred geometry of the planets and stars as they move in the sky.

Harmonious and Challenging Aspects

Challenging aspects, also called "hard" aspects, include the 1st, 2nd, 4th, 8th and 16th harmonics. Hard aspects have an element of force attributed to them. They confront us and may even push us to change. Transits forming a hard aspect are rarely subtle and are typically experienced externally as well as internally. With challenging transits, we tend to have the experience whether we are open to it or not. If we are open to the experience and not resisting, then a challenging transit or natal aspect can be experienced with grace and ease.

Harmonious aspects, also called "flowing", "easy", "graceful" or "soft" aspects, include the 3rd and 6th harmonics. Harmonious transits may come and go without notice. Often it is up to us to access the gifts of the transit and intentionally receive and accept what is being offered. If the transit is a flowing one, we may want to actively solicit the planets involved so as to reap the benefits that are available. If we do not avail ourselves to the opportunities presented with these flowing and easy aspects and transits, then we may find that we have given the Universe the message that we are not interested in our personal growth or evolution. Then we may find ourselves in a place that feels stuck, stagnant or depressed.

Octaves

Music and astrology must be very connected. The Titius-Bode Law, which was used to predict the distance between the planets and the Sun, was developed using the Major Scale in music. In astrology what we call harmonics is basically the same thing as in music. In music, a harmonic is the angular relationship between two notes while in astrology it is the angular relationship between two planets—both being simple geometric ratios. In astrology we also use the concept of octaves to talk about how two planets are related to each other. In music, an octave is the same note only a certain frequency higher or lower. In astrology we consider the vibrational quality of some planets to be similar, only higher or lower. Mercury is the lower octave planet of Uranus. Venus is the lower octave planet of Neptune. Mars is the lower octave planet of Pluto.

Mercury and **Uranus** are both about the mind, communication and understanding. While Mercury is about how an individual thinks, how the mind actually works in relationship to the brain, and how communication occurs on a mundane level, Uranus speaks to the concept of there being one great mind from which all ideas spring forth. Uranus is the higher mind and the keeper of all information. Uranus represents the ideas that come from out of the box, out of the culture, out of this world. Align Mercury and Uranus and we have brilliance, high levels of intelligence that can be communicated along with creative ideas. Mis-align these two and we have an over-active or under-active mind and mental instability.

With **Venus** and **Neptune** both being planets of love—Venus about human relationships and Neptune about relationship to the Divine—we are asked to open our hearts. We must increase our ability to love or we will suffer. The heart wants to expand, wants to feel new things, and wants to fall in love. We are also called to open our hearts to others, to be compassionate and caring and to honor the Divine within each of us. Align these two and we have great works of art, true love, deep compassion and profound understanding of the human condition. Mis-align these two and we have an overdeveloped romantic imagination, a distorted view of love or an excessive longing for pleasure.

With **Mars** and **Pluto** in an octave relationship we move through another twist of the wheel in evolution. There is a challenge here to change at a deep level—to transform how we use (or abuse) power. Mars and Pluto are planets of desire and power. Mars is the principle of activated power that can be used to express ourselves in the world. Pluto is the principle of power that transforms at the very core of life. Align these two and we have the super heroes, magicians, high priestesses, atomic energy, profound relationships and great discoveries. Mis-align these two and we have wars, legal battles, genetic mutation, and hormonal overdrive.

Note: Within the Mercury-Uranus octave, it is

interesting to note that Mercury takes 88 days to get around the Sun while Uranus takes 84 years to get around the Sun. The relationship of an Earth day to an Earth year is like a spinning top; both originate with the same force. The hand spins the top and it both rotates and revolves. The force relates both the rotation, a day, to the revolution, a year. While it might seem, at one level, that we are comparing apples and oranges, we are given a glimpse of the mystical patterns in the universe.

Along the same lines, for every two Venus days, the Earth revolves around the Sun three times. For every two Neptune days, the Earth rotates three times. Thus we have some kind of a 2/3 harmonic relationship with the Venus-Neptune octave.

Also, Mars and Pluto have an interesting relationship as well, though it is a bit of a stretch. Mars revolves around the Sun every 687 days, while Pluto rotates on its axis every 6.4 days, a factor of 100.

The Void-of-Course Moon

Every time the Moon changes signs, which occurs about every 2½ days, there is a period of time between the last major aspect to the moon and the moon entering the next sign. This time period is when the moon is void-of-course. It is as if the aspects to the moon keep the moon in connection to the whole.

The general astrological counsel for the void-of-course

moon is to avoid making commitments, signing contracts, making important decisions and buying things, since it is likely that the outcome will be different than expected or hoped. Often what we do during a void-of-course moon goes into the void. We buy the sweater we wind up returning. The contract turns out null and void. So during this time it may be wise to avoid things we do not want to be voided. I say *may* because there is a flow to the universe and there are things that want to be done during this time. In my experience, I usually do not know what it is that wants to happen during this time so that the less attachment I have to my own agenda the more "right" the time goes. In the process of letting go of my own agenda, opportunities and synchronicities appear and then, without prior intent, I find myself meeting the man of my dreams (yes, this really happened during a void-of-course moon), finding the perfect raincoat for my son or writing the best newsletter ever. I often have readings during this time since it seems to be a good time for channeling, magic and having hair-raising insights.

Timing a Transit

The planets are the archetypes of teachers, masters and guides. Their kingdom is the kingdom we live in during their transit. We are asked to accept their teachings. Resistance usually makes things more difficult. Depending on the harmonic of the transit, our will may play significantly or have little effect. Often we are simply asked to accept what is being shown to us.

The planets move around the Sun (at least we still think they do) and each has their own orbit and speed and slant and density and proclivities. To find peace, we must accept and honor all planets just as we must accept and honor everything about ourselves and this world.

Since we are living on Earth, this planet is our reference point. We could take the reference point of the Sun but then we would need to keep journeying there and I have heard it is quite an unfriendly environment for these three-dimensional forms we are carrying. So the planets move. They move in some direction and with some speed. All of the planets move around the Sun with a consistent speed and in the same direction. However, our unique perspective from this planet means that the planets don't always appear to be moving in the same direction or with a consistent speed. Have you ever been on a train when the train next to you starts to pull ahead, but it feels like the train you are on is going backwards? This is like the *retrograde* motion of the planets. The retrograding planet simply appears to be moving backwards in relationship to our planet, because our planet is not actually in the center of the solar system. The energy of a planet varies depending on whether it is moving forward, called *direct*, or retrograde. When a planet appears to be standing still, i.e. when it is changing directions, that is its most potent moment. This is a moment to be savored and acknowledged. This is when the planet is Queen of the sky. We say the planet is *stationing*, although its effect is usually anything but stationary.

Due to this retrograde phenomenon, the other planet's apparent *speed* also changes. The other planet appears to slow down before going retrograde, appears to stop, turn around, go retrograde, gradually pick up speed, slow down again, stop, turn around again, and go direct, picking up speed until it is time to apparently go retrograde, again. Each planet has its own momentum. Some go retrograde often. Some rarely. Naturally, the Sun and the Moon never go retrograde. Their speeds are fairly consistent though not entirely. The Moon picks up speed at various points in its cycle, due the fact that its orbit is not perfectly circular.

The speed of a planet is significant in its effect (or in its perceived effect.) The slower the planet is moving the more likely the transit is to produce the typical results of the transit. Planets that move slowly tend to stimulate deeper transformations. Since some planets ride a point for over a year, we have plenty of time to acknowledge and get the picture of what is going on. We have ample opportunity to learn the lesson we are being offered. In contrast, a planet that moves over a point in a day or so rarely gives us the chance to know what is going on. Often these quicker moving planets serve as a *trigger* for a longer transit taking place. We can time the likely events of a transit from the triggers occurring.

In order to understand the timing of a transit, we also need to know the orb of the transit. *Orbs, or orbs of influence, are the range of degrees in which we observe the greatest effect of the transit.* While orbs have been determined through centuries of observation, different astrologers use different orbs.

Guidelines to Timing a Transit

1.   Use an ephemeris, astrology software or an astrologer to find out what transits you are experiencing. An ephemeris is a book of tables of where the planets are on any given day. It is an essential book for anyone studying astrology. *Journey-work of the Stars: An Astrology Workbook*, my first book, offers an introduction to finding transits using an ephemeris.

2.   If we are under a **hard transit**, which includes harmonics 1, 2, 4, and 8, we will experience the transit more intensely. The transit will be more confrontational. The lower the harmonic the more powerful the transit will be. In particular, harmonics 1, 2 and 4 almost always produce the effect of the transit. These harmonics include the conjunction ($0°$), opposition ($180°$) and square ($90°$). The 8th harmonic includes all of those aspects with the addition of the semi-square ($45°$) and the sesquiquadrate ($135°$). These additional minor aspects will give a subtler experience.

3.   If we are under a **soft transit**, harmonics 3 and 6, we are opened to the possibilities of the transit. The transit acts in harmony with our purpose. The 3rd harmonic includes the conjunctions ($0°$) and the trine ($120°$).

4.   If we are under quintiles and septiles, harmonics 5 and 7, the transit is experienced more internally. The stress of the aspect pushes us to grow.

5.   For timing, use the orbs given under each planet as a beginning barometer.

a.   When an outer planet (Chiron, Uranus, Neptune and Pluto) transits a personal point (Sun, Moon, Ascendant, Descendant, MC or IC), extend the orb a few degrees. When a transitional planet (Jupiter and Saturn), transits an inner planet extend the orb a degree or two.

b.   Extend the orb when the transiting planet is going retrograde back and forth over the natal planet.

c.   Outer and transitional planets transiting natal planets will have the greatest impact when it is triggered by another transit.

d.   Multiple planets transiting a natal planet will extend the orb and timing.

e.   A **trigger planet** is the planet that sets off an event or experience of an outer planet transit more intensely. Pay particular attention to Mars as a trigger for Pluto transits, Venus as a trigger for Neptune transits, and Mercury as a trigger for Uranus transits. The Sun and Moon, particularly New and Full Moons are also powerful triggers. Any inner planet that is stationing operates as a powerful trigger. The more planets transiting a natal planet, the more fated and predictable our experience will be. Eclipses (when the nodes are aligned with a full or new moon) are very activating triggers. An eclipse transiting a natal planet that is already being transited by an outer planet can produce profound results within a six-month range.

6.   Saturn, Chiron, Uranus and sometimes Jupiter will transit a planet three times. The *first* time the transit occurs, we are awakened to its effects. Sometimes this is a

harsh awakening. The first transit opens our eyes to the issue that requires growth. If all of life is a path of awakening, the transits are the pre-programmed opportunities for us to work out whatever is getting in the way to that awakening. When the transit first comes in, it is bringing forth something in us that has been dormant— something latent or hidden. The event that arises in the presence of dormant issue may seem random, but nothing is random. Even this issue, that we have so carefully dodged our whole life is part of the big picture of who we are. Each transit helps us wake up an aspect of ourselves and see that aspect from a new vantage point. When the transit begins whether we like what is happening or not, we are often caught off-guard. It is the beauty and the challenge of the transits. Even when we know they are coming, what actually shows up is often a surprise. The *second* transit offers us a chance to make decisions in alignment with the transit. During the second transit, we integrate and move into rhythm with the transit. Once the initial shock of the first transit is over, the second transit supports us in diving deeper into the truth of who we are. We can see the gifts of the events surrounding the planets in transit. The *third* time the planet transits we are able to come to resolution and completion. The more we are open and accepting of the shifts in the beginning of the transit, the easier the rest of the transit is. When we resist the transit during the first two passes, the third time the transit occurs we may experience the most unpleasant aspects of the transiting planet. It is as if the transit has a mission and it will accomplish this mission whether we like it or not. The challenges that happen at the end of a transit may reflect our denial or resistance to the necessary change. More often, we experience a sense of accomplishment, resolution or peace at this time. Each transiting planet has a reward for us. In the end, accepting the gift is often the best way to move forward into the next transit.

7.   Neptune and Pluto usually transit a planet or point five times. The first time is the wake-up call, often harsh and unexpected. The second reminds us that this isn't going away anytime soon. The third begins to help us to heal and accept our new reality. By the time the fourth transit occurs, we have most likely accepted the work of the transit. Now we can take steps forward to align the lesson with the new life that is beginning to emerge. The fifth time brings the gift. Pluto opens us to power and riches, however we define power and riches. Neptune opens us to love and peace.

8.   When an inner planet (Mars, Venus and Mercury) goes retrograde it can transit a natal planet three times. In this case, greater consideration and significance is given to the transit than usual. The typically fast moving inner planet can act as powerfully by transit as Jupiter or Saturn.

9.   When a planet stations transiting a natal planet within one degree of orb, it is a particularly powerful transit and is more likely to produce the expected results of the transit.

Order of Observing the Transits

1.   I always start with Saturn. It isn't the most important planet, nor does it create the deepest change, but it anchors us in our version of reality. Saturn transits are the most predictable and most universally experienced.

~Note conjunctions, oppositions and squares.

~Note which house it is in.

~If we are before our first Saturn return (at 29 years old), we tend to experience Saturn transits with a greater degree of confrontation and challenge. After the Saturn return, it is often easier to assimilate and use Saturn transits to our benefit.

2.   Note Jupiter transits by conjunction, opposition and house placement. Jupiter points out the opportunities in our life.

3.   Note Pluto transits where the deepest change is occurring. In particular, pay attention to Mars as a trigger planet.

4.   Note Neptune transits, particularly Neptune oppose, conjunct or square the Sun or Moon.

5.   Note Uranus transits to Sun, Moon, Ascendant, and Descendant, particularly conjunction, opposition and square. Also look at where Uranus trines to support change in our lives.

6.   Note where the Eclipses land and if they transit the Nodes, the Sun, Moon, Ascendant, or Midheaven.

7.   Note Pluto, Neptune or Uranus trining Sun, Moon, Ascendant or Midheaven.

8. Note Pluto, Neptune, Uranus, Saturn, Jupiter conjunct, oppose, square or trine Mercury, Venus or Mars.

9. Note Chiron conjunct a personal planet. Note Chiron return between 50 - 51 years old.

10. Note Eclipses transiting anything else in the chart.

11. Now look at minor transits, including sextiles and quincunxes. Most important are the outer planets transiting the personal points of the Sun, Moon, Ascendant, Descendant and Nodes.

Timing Specific Events

Meeting a significant other

Almost everyone who isn't in love wants to know when they will find love (even if they don't want to ask). Here is a general list of transits I look for in the order I use:

1. Naibod Secondary Progressed Venus conjunct Sun or Progressed Sun conjunct Venus. I know we haven't covered this in this manual, but that's where I start.

2. Chiron conjunct Venus.

3. Jupiter moving through the 7th house.

4. Neptune conjunct, oppose, square, quincunx or trine Venus—however, I recommend caution with this transit. The relationship isn't always what it seems to be. Wait until the transit is done until combining finances or signing a contract.

5. Chiron trine or quincunx Venus.

6.   Jupiter, Chiron or Neptune conjunct, oppose or trine the ruler of the 7th house.

7.   Uranus trine Venus.

8.   Neptune, Uranus, Chiron or Jupiter conjunct or trine a planet in the 7th house.

9.   New or Full Moon on the person's birthday. The Solar Return chart will then be a New or Full Moon. This opens the possibility for love during the entire year following that birthday.

Moving

Moving tends to be easier to predict than love:

1.   Jupiter in the 4th house.

2.   Jupiter or Uranus conjunct, oppose, square or trine the Moon.

(Unless I see Saturn transit the Moon or Saturn in the 4th house, I tend to think it's fine to move. Moving isn't such a big deal these days and can be supported through any transit to the Moon.)

3.   Pluto conjunct, oppose or square the Moon. This can support a big move, perhaps even to another country.

Vocational Development

1.   Saturn through the houses.

The career cycle is a 29-year cycle that accurately follows Saturn through the houses. Each house is a stage. Saturn moves through each stage (house) for two to three years. See Saturn through the houses. This anchors the career cycle.

2.   Jupiter transiting the Midheaven opens up job opportunities.

3.   Uranus on the Midheaven indicates changes to career.

4.   Note Neptune and Pluto on the Midheaven for deeper changes in career.

5.   Note any planet transiting the 10th house, particularly if there are planets in the 10th house. Note the timing of outer planets conjunct, oppose, square or trine a planet in the 10th house.

6.   Note outer planets transiting Saturn.

7.   Note transits to the ruler of the Midheaven.

Children

Unlike with other transits, when to have children is strongly affected by a person's age, particularly for women. It is generally accepted in the medical community that it becomes more difficult for a woman to conceive and birth children the nearer to fifty we get. As astrologers, we get to observe a bigger picture, while honoring the very real human experience. We usually don't have to remind women of their biological clock.

With this in mind, we can offer a perspective on timing.

1.   Jupiter moving through the 4th and 5th houses is the easiest time for conception and birth. Jupiter opens the opportunity to increase our home and family size. In fact, this transit is so likely to bring in children that I often warn those who don't want children to be extra careful to use contraception during these two years.

2.   Jupiter trining the Moon is a graceful support for conception and birth.

3.   I look at the cycle of Saturn through the houses. If Saturn is moving through the 7th through the 11th houses, we tend to be more focused on worldly experiences rather than creating and focusing on children and home. However, the exception to this is when a person's life calling is to have children. For this exception I note benefics (Venus, Jupiter or Mercury) in the 5th house, especially a bright moon in the 5th. A Cancer Sun with a strong Moon in the birth chart supports having a family as a life calling. There are many ways to see this in a chart. Pluto or Saturn in the 5th house can delay or obstruct having children.

4.   Saturn transiting the 5th house can be a two-and-a-half year window where it is more challenging to conceive. Our living children tend to need more from us during this time.

5.   Saturn conjunct the Moon tends to be a more difficult year to conceive. Saturn asks the Moon to turn inward, to contract and to work the foundation.

Health

First off, I rarely predict an illness using Western astrology. I have seen people sail effortlessly through the hardest of health transits. So much depends on our constitution and outlook on life. My intention in using astrology is to bring forth the highest in a person. Needlessly worrying about an illness tends to fly in contradiction to bringing forth the highest in us. Only when I see multiple health transits do I make health suggestions—and the health suggestions are almost always a recommendation to see a health professional. Unless we have a license to practice medicine or health counseling, I suggest proceeding with caution in this aspect of astrology.

With that cautionary note, here are transits that affect our health.

1.   Saturn moving through the 6th house suggests a time to focus on our daily rhythm—when and how we eat, sleep and exercise. We may get signs that it is time to change a long-term habit.

2.   Pluto, Neptune or Uranus conjunct, oppose or square a planet in the 6th house. The 6th house is the house of incarnation—this is where and how the soul bonds to the body at birth. If there are challenging planets in the 6th (Pluto, Uranus or Saturn), we may have had a challenging birth. Sometimes our soul doesn't fully bond with our body and health issues arise from this challenge. Again, this is not a rule but an indication in the case that a person is already experiencing health challenges.

3.   Chiron conjunct, oppose or square the Sun or Moon may bring on a healing crisis. This crisis often triggers an old wound and then supports deeper healing. I tend to think of this transit as supportive for deeper healing.

4.   Neptune conjunct, oppose or square the Sun can weaken our immune system. Since this transit supports us in doing more spiritual work, the focus isn't on worldly life. Ergo, the worldly life needs can stress our systems. If we allow for the soul searching that this transit enjoys, then our physical health is less likely to weaken.

5.   Saturn in the 12th or Saturn conjunct, oppose or square the Sun or Moon indicates a time when we may be moving at a slower pace. We may feel lower energy. Life slows down so that we can pay attention to our significant Saturn lesson in life. Simply allowing the slow down, saying No, and cutting back activities is supportive during these transits.

Money, Wealth and Investing

1.   Saturn through the 2nd house can be experienced as a crunch time. Saturn is helping us get clear about what we really want and it does this through limiting us, usually financially. Time to simplify. At the same time, long-term investments made at this time tend to gain steadily.

2.   Jupiter through the 2nd and 8th houses tends to support greater ease in acquiring resources.

3.   Pluto, Neptune and Uranus moving through the 2nd or 8th houses suggest long-term focus on finances. Look for Jupiter, Saturn, stationing Mars or stationing Venus triggering these long-term transits to indicate changes in financial situations. Uranus can always go either way. Pluto tends to create loss followed by gain. Neptune tends to indicate a lack of clarity and misuse of funds. Neptune moving through the 2nd house is about learning to trust that the Universe has our back.

4.   Look at transits to the rulers of the 2nd and 8th house.

5.   Look at transits to planets in the 2nd and 8th houses.

6.   Note the house Saturn is in.

The Sun Transits

Perceived Effect: The Sun sheds light on an issue. A lesson becomes visible. A new perspective offers a chance for joy and hope. Sun radiates warmth and life. A Sun transit brings the transited planet into the light and shows us how the positive side of the planet.

Lessons:

The Sun teaches us to look on the bright side of Life. It offers us the understanding that our attitude impacts, if not wholly creates, the situations in our life. The Sun is the vibrancy and essence of who we are. When the Sun in our natal chart is transited, the change and lesson is indeed significant and affects the very core of our being. When the Sun is the transiting planet, for the week that is shines its light, we see the transited planet more clearly. We are offered insight and clarity about the work and purpose of the planet being highlighted. In fact, the Sun acts like a giant highlighter, going along and pointing out quickly each planet and its purpose. Since the Sun does the same revolution every year, we get to explore every Sun transit once every year. It is the transits of the Sun that give us the yearly rhythm of life. If we like the first week of fall or that week in February when the days really feel like they are getting longer, or particularly dislike a particular time of the year, look to the Sun and see what it is transiting during that time of year. The early parts of November are usually a challenging time for me. It could just be how dark it gets in the northwest in late autumn or it could have something to do with the Sun transiting my 8th house during that time.

Retrograde: Never

Orbit: The Earth takes a year to get around the Sun. From our perspective on Earth, it looks like it takes the Sun a year to get around the Earth.

Orb: 7°

Time it takes: The Earth always moves at the same rate in relation to the Sun, about one degree a day. This transit takes two weeks. So celebrate your birthday for a week before and a week after. ☺

~~~~~~~~~~

Sun/Sun
Our birthday, among other days of the year, is a day when light is shed on who we are. Our resonance is clearer. We feel more radiant and with greater openness to life. This is a good day to set intentions for the coming year, as is a common tradition on one's birthday.

Read *99 Keys to a Creative Life: Spiritual, Intuitive, and Awareness Practices for Personal Fulfillment by Melissa Harris*

Sun/Moon
Light is shed on our emotional state. Our conditioned responses to life become clearer to us. We can become more aware of unconscious responses to life's dilemmas.

Read *The Temple of My Familiar by Alice Walker*

Sun/Mercury
Light is shed on how we think and communicate. We may become more aware of our unique communication patterns. Our thinking can be clearer. This is usually a good day to make decisions and sign contracts, especially during the time that the Sun conjuncts Mercury.

Read *A Moveable Feast by Ernest Hemingway*

Sun/Venus

A beautiful aspect for creative endeavors and opening to passion. Live a little—open to beauty and your unique creative expression. These days are often days filled with love and support if we dare to receive it.

Read *Gone with the Wind by Margaret Mitchell*

Sun/Mars

Most of us can use a little added energy boost, and this transit can put an extra pep in our step, an added jive to our drive. A good time to be active and use the energy to get stuff done. If you feel extra agitation right now, turn to physical work or exercise.

Read *Yes: Screenplay and Notes by Sally Potter*

Sun/Jupiter

This may trigger opportunities and openings for growth. Something wants to grow. We may feel that we get more out of life. Take this as a sign to create something different in your life rather than feel something is lacking. Take a road trip or read a new book. Open to the fullness of life.

Read *Eat, Pray, Love by Elizabeth Gilbert*

Sun/Nodes

During this time, we have light shed on our soul work. Pay attention for signs. When the Sun is conjunct the South Node, we are offered a chance to complete some aspect of our past life identity. Look at this time as a chance for completion. When the Sun is on the North Node, we are opened up to our soul path. People born on these dates tend to be good for our souls. I like to pay special attention to that week in which the Sun is conjunct my North Node, as a time when I am getting good and clear messages from the Universe.

Read *Letters to a Young Poet by Rainer Maria Rilke*

Sun/Saturn

Our core karmic lessons are highlighted—especially where we limit ourselves. We can also see more clearly our path in the world. We may feel more ambitious or directed. Use this energy to overcome an obstacle or interference.

Read *Beloved by Toni Morrison*

Sun/Chiron

Our wounding becomes clearer and we can work on healing during these days. Open to the possibility of healing rather than a crisis. Take some time to take care of yourself by cooking a good meal, or getting a massage or energy work session.

Read *How to Cook Everything: The Basics, All You Need to Make Great Food by Mark Bittman or any cookbook*

Sun/Uranus

Where we typically feel out of control in our lives, we may feel added stress or anxiety. We can feel excited and hopeful or we can feel scared—our choice. This transit is meant to bring us alive. Allow the free flow of energy through your cells.

Read *Making the Gods Work for You: The Astrological Language of the Psyche by Caroline W. Casey*

Sun/Neptune

Our visions and spiritual lives get an added boost. Pay attention to dreams, they can carry important messages about our life energy and attitudes about life. Follow your intuition more and allow the days around this transit to unfold without agenda (as much as possible).

Read *Memories, Dreams, Reflections by C.G. Jung*

Sun/Pluto

This transit shows us how we are evolving this lifetime. While this may not be felt overly, we may see signs that reflect progress on our paths.

Read *A Brief History of Everything by Ken Wilber*

Sun/Ascendant

The Sun sheds its light on our purpose within the larger world. We are more visible to others. Our achievements shine brighter and we can receive more support than we are used to. Others see our best selves.

Read *The Secret by Rhonda Byrne*

Sun/Midheaven

Light is shed on our work in the world. We may have helpful insights that show us the path and light the way. We may also see more clearly what needs to change in our home. Take some time to clear out a space in your home for journaling and ritual. Then ask for clarity about your vocation and calling in this life.

Read *If You Don't Know Where You're Going, You'll Probably End Up Somewhere Else by David Campbell, Ph.D.*

~~~~~~~~~~~

Stones for support in a Sun transit:

To support us during a *Sun* transit, **Ruby** and **Almondine** can boost us. **Tiger's Eye** is also a stone that supports us in feeling more vital and in bringing in more solar fire. **Calcite** can mitigate the difficult transits of the Sun helping us to ground, focus and feel more supported. **Aquamarine** can cool the solar fire if the heat is too much.

New & Full Moon Transits

Perceived Effect: The Moon rules how we process the stimuli, internal or external, that is going on in our lives. It rules our emotional bodies and the health of our overall systems. The Moon will only transit another planet for several hours and yet can be observed to be highly influential as a trigger for longer-term transits.

Lessons: The Moon rules our emotions and teaches us to feel and perceive even that which we can't see with our eyes. It helps us to align our intuition, accepting that not everything can be experienced through our five senses.

Retrograde: Never

Orbit: The Moon always shows us the same face because it takes 27.3 days for the Moon to rotate on its axis the same time it takes to revolve around our planet. The Lunar month (the synodic cycle of the Sun and Moon) varies between 29.3 and 29.8 days.

Orb: 7°

Time it takes: The New Moon transit applies for the entire lunar month.

Transits of the Moon trigger events or experiences related to the longer term transits occurring. In general, a transit from the Moon only lasts for several hours. Important transits that I like to note are:

1) When the **Moon conjuncts the North Node**— This is a time when advice, signs, information or experiences are in alignment with our soul purpose. I trust these signs more when the Moon is joined to my North Node. Alternatively, when the Moon is conjunct the South Node, we are more likely to get messages that support old and familiar ways of being. This is a time for completing old business and putting things to rest. I hold advice or information that I get at this time with a light hand.

2) When the **Moon conjuncts the Natal Moon**— This is what is called the Lunar Return. A chart drawn up for the moment when the Moon conjuncts the natal Moon is a chart used for seeing into the next 28 days—our own personal beginning of the month or the lunar cycle.

3) **New and Full Moons which conjunct points in the natal chart** are important and often significant triggers for events. New Moons show times for beginning while Full Moons show times when the intensity of the issues at hand can be felt full tilt. Full Moons open and transform the points they access. New Moons help us to set ourselves in a new direction.

4) **Solar and Lunar Eclipses** are very important celestial events. The earliest recordings of astrology are the observations and events that occur during them. Take the New Moon (Solar Eclipse) and intensify it many fold. Take the Full Moon (Lunar Eclipse) and intensify its effects many times. Eclipses are known to stir up trouble, passion, disruption, craziness, love, and put life a little more on the edge—or a lot more on the edge.

~~~~~~~~~~

New Moon/Sun
Set your sights on who you want to be, your personality, your individuality, your own personal style.

New Moon/Moon
This often begins a lunar cycle of deep emotional changes. We can more easily change habits, understand rote ways of

being and bring into awareness areas that have felt hidden, buried and inaccessible.

New Moon/Mercury
Get ready for a month of mental activity. New ideas can rise up. Communication can flow easily. Reading, thinking, learning are all highlighted activities.

New Moon/Venus
The potential beginning of a love affair—with someone, something, or some new way of being. Time to take up a new hobby, start a new garden, open to receiving from the world. Financially, this may be a good month if we pay attention to our values and be cautious not to over-spend.

New Moon/Mars
Time to initiate and take action in some area where there has been stuck-ness or uncertainty. When we make a decision and set an intention, the Universe is then able to collude with us and support our direction if it is what we need. This is an excellent time to take action towards an area that is dearly important or needed for soul or bodily survival.

New Moon/Jupiter
Time to focus on growth. Time to turn our sights on an area in our lives that desires expansion. Open to learning and travel.

New Moon/Nodes
The New Moon conjunct the North Node supports us in

moving forward with our life. When this is within one degree, this is an important Lunar Month for us. We get messages and signs that support us in moving more clearly into our soul purpose. When the New Moon joins our South Node, we begin a month that supports completion of past life work. We may find that we are supported in looking at an old pattern so that we can shift it.

New Moon/Saturn

This is an important month where karmic lessons will be highlighted. We will likely be asked to make a careful and clear decision. This is time to cut back, curtail or commit to an area of focus.

New Moon/Chiron

An excellent time to look at wounds of old that need healing. A good time to focus on physical as well as emotional and spiritual healing.

New Moon/Uranus

This may be a cycle where it is difficult to understand what is going on. We may experience a greater degree of chaos. On the other hand we can make changes now with great ease. Trying to hold on will upset an already upset Uranus. Enjoy the excitement of change without knowing where it is leading.

New Moon/Neptune

A month of powerful dreams. A good time to focus on spiritual endeavors, communicating with the ancestors, meditating or praying. There is a great need to trust right now because things may seem unclear if we are trying to use logic or reason to interpret the events in our lives.

New Moon/ Pluto
Begins a month of deep transformation—sometimes so deep we can't even see it or understand it. This is a month to honor death and transformation without clinging or holding onto some cherished idea of how things "should" be. There are no "shoulds" with Pluto.

New Moon/Ascendant
This is an auspicious New Moon for changing our appearance, starting a new phase in our life, enhancing our self-image or exhibiting a creative piece we have done.

New Moon/Midheaven
We may begin a new course of work at this time. It begins a month that is good for moving or taking on new work.

~~~~~~~~~~

Full Moon/Sun
We can have greater clarity about our path and identity at this time. We may choose to make a change in our appearance or have new insights into who we are.

Full Moon/Moon
During this month, we may see very clearly our path and can trust our instincts. Our senses may be more heightened than usual. We may understand things that have been mysteries to us in the past. We may also be more emotional or easily set off during this month.

Full Moon/Mercury

Wisdom and logic combined can support us in making better decisions. We may find ourselves communicating more directly or emotionally during this month.

Full Moon/Venus

Look out for love that might surprise you this month. The Moon pushes us to open to experience more sensuality and pleasure. Creativity may flow through us more fully.

Full Moon/Mars

If there is something that requires courage, this is a good month to move forward with it. We may also feel a bit more agitated or stressed. Take care to not overdo it, since we may not know our own strength during this time.

Full Moon/Jupiter

Jupiter helps us see the big picture and so does the Full Moon. This Full Moon highlights travel and expanding our horizons. Openly celebrate something in your life that excites you. Say Yes to a new possibility. Do something that gets you out of your regular routine and trust the wisdom that easily comes your way.

Full Moon/Nodes

This entire Lunar Month highlights the mysterious work of the soul. Signs and synchronicities abound. If the Full Moon joins the North Node, light is shed on your soul direction and supports movement towards that which opens up new paths, even if it uncomfortable. If the Full Moon joins the South Node, we can clearly see something old that has been blocking us on our path to our deepest happiness. Time to let it go. The Full Moon squaring the Nodes shows us something that needs to change in our life, some condition that is hindering us on our soul path. First we must face it and then we can transform it.

Full Moon/Saturn

Since Saturn is the portal into our lessons and blocks, the Full Moon transiting Saturn gives us a front row seat to any belief that holds us in limitation. If we think we aren't enough, or loveable, or smart enough, or that this world is hard, then we will get a golden opportunity to look squarely at this belief. Often the opportunity shows up as what seems like a validation of this negative self-belief. In reality, someone or some situation is merely imitating what we are saying to ourselves and offering us a chance to correct that unconscious voice. We have a choice in this month to change a core pattern that has been running us.

Full Moon/Chiron

In Chiron, we explore the core wound that begs to be healed. The Full Moon helps us to understand and see the wound. It may trigger a healing crisis—emotional or physical—but ultimately helps us heal something deeper. Like lancing an abscess, it's not always easy, but once done the healing can happen quickly.

Full Moon/Uranus

The Full Moon dancing on our Uranus helps us understand some underlying anxiety, some aspect of our life that seems out of our control and triggers nervousness.

Generations hold the fears of the time they are born in. The Full Moon can help us see these invisible influences and question ideas that our generation and previous generations have come to accept, perhaps wrongly, as fact.

Full Moon/Neptune

Neptune holds the unsolved mysteries of our time, the cultural cover-ups and the hidden agendas. The Full Moon can shed light on the effects these mysteries have on our psyches, especially fears and phobias that inhibit our free expression. We may be more sensitive this month or more inclined to delve deeper into our psychological issues.

Full Moon/Pluto

With the ability to see more clearly the underlying fears that have kept us from our fullest expression, we can take a courageous leap forward. Look hard and long this month at how you give your power away to others or to your falsely perceived limitations. This crazy world needs all of us to transform into more loving and awake individuals. This is a good month for a deep healing session, workshop or inner quest intensive.

~~~~~~~~~~

Stones for support in Moon transit:
The *Moon* likes **Moonstone,** naturally, which helps us get in touch with our feminine side, nurturance and fertility. **Opal** helps us release emotion. Pearls are another support during lunar transits.

Mercury Transits

Perceived Effect: Mercury tends to inspire or diminish clarity of mind and effective communication. Mercury supports analysis, concrete thinking, and expression through language.

Lessons: This trickster, this planet of impish pranks, this androgynous archetype of clever thinking, this messenger of the Gods, teaches us to lighten up and see the humor in life. It shows us how to learn, how to listen, how to respond, how to speak clearly. Mercury teaches us how to get along and connect with others on a day-to-day basis. It asks us to open to new ideas and new ways of doing things. It challenges us to move out of ruts and patterns of thought and expand our horizons, at least mentally. Since it often moves too fast to have a significant effect, we often get its lessons during the retrograde period when it slows down.

Retrograde: Mercury goes retrograde three times a year for three weeks at a time. These retrograde periods are important to note since Mercury rules the mind, the mental realm, communication, thought, and short distance travel. During retrograde periods, the effect is that our minds work differently. We tend to process things more internally first, thus experiencing a delay in the way our thoughts come across. It is easier to miscommunicate or mis-hear another's communication when we are processing information differently. Often we experience delays and general mess-ups if we are pushing or expending effort.

While it is retrograde, Mercury is pulling us into a more reflective space. It is offering us a time to look inward, to reorganize, to slow down our often overly active minds, and to focus on creative endeavors.

There are many wonderful things to do during a Mercury retrograde period. First of all, I understand that it takes 21 days to change a habit, the exact time span that Mercury goes retrograde. So ceasing a habit, creating a new habit, healing an addiction, or making a lifestyle change are all highlighted and have a greater chance for success if done during the Mercury retrograde period. We can alter patterns of thought during this fruitful inner time. This can be a creative time, especially for intellectually stimulating creative projects like writing. This can be a difficult time to *willfully* move forward with projects and time-lines.

Orbit: It takes 88 earth days for Mercury to get around the Sun. Mercury goes retrograde three times a year for about 21 days. The synodic cycle of Mercury is 122 days. The synodic cycle is measured from the midpoint time of one retrograde period until the midpoint time of the next retrograde period.

Orb: 3° If Mercury goes retrograde over a planet, transiting that planet three times, the transit is in effect for the entire time Mercury is retrograde, plus three degrees on either side.

Time it takes: Mercury's speed in relation to Earth varies quite a lot since it goes retrograde so often, when it slows down, turns around, speeds up a little, then turns around again—and by the time it gets up to full speed again, it's almost time to turn around again. At full-speed forward, Mercury takes two or three days to transit a point. During a retrograde period, it could take two months to move back and forth over a point.

~~~~~~~~~~~

Mercury/Sun

A conjunction of Mercury to our Sun usually occurs around our birthday time and honors the use of logic and

55

reason to be able to support our overall well-being. When the Sun and Mercury are within ten degrees of each other, this is considered combustion and can be a challenging time for Mercury, since objectivity is often lost. Other transits of Mercury to the Sun are assets for focus, logic, and the ability to make decisions with the force of ego.

Read *The Power of Positive Thinking by Norman Vincent Peale*

Mercury/Mercury
This marks a time of increased mental activity. We are triggered to communicate more and with greater keenness. We may find ourselves overwhelmed with thoughts and ideas. Take some time to write down ideas and thoughts at this time. In order to move through overwhelm, get physical—dance, walk, move your body.

Read *On Writing: A Memoir of the Craft by Stephen King* (A generous work of art that will get you inspired to write your own Great Book.)

Mercury/Venus
The mind wants to understand what is going in our relationships. The mind wants to mingle with our creative world. Our mind wants to figure out financial strategies. Let the mind have a go at it. Honor the ability of the mind to think through a problem or a potential improvement point. We can be mentally clearer and more creative during this aspect.

Read *The Shipping News by Annie Proulx* (It's the last page that gets me to reread this classic.)

Mercury/Mars

With Mercury ruling thought and Mars ruling action, this is a time when we may feel spurred to action by a thought or understanding. We may be extra impulsive during this transit. Remember to wait a beat before doing something rash.

Read *The Mists of Avalon by Marion Zimmerman Bradshaw*

Mercury/Jupiter

This is an excellent time to ponder the Great Books. Knowledge seeking, travel, exploring and any learning are highlighted during this aspect of journeying.

Read *In Search of the Miraculous by Pyotr Ouspenskii*

Mercury/Nodes

Extra emphasis on our soul direction supports our ability to communicate and share our truth. When Mercury transits the Nodes, we find ourselves in an inquiry into what really matters. It is time to ask deep questions about our soul purpose. We have a chance to get clearer about our direction and what really makes us happy.

Read *Alchemy of Nine Dimensions: Decoding the Vertical Axis, Crop Circles, and the Mayan Calendar by Barbara Hand Clow with Gerry Clow*

Mercury/Saturn

Setting clear boundaries and being the "author" of our lives is important "write" now. We are asked to accept responsibility for our thoughts, ideas and communications. We can also understand to a greater degree what our core life lessons are and why we are struggling with a certain area of life.

Read *Writing Down the Bones: Freeing the Writer Within by Natalie Goldberg*

Mercury/Chiron

There is a wound that we are all born with and it differs from being to being. This is a time to understand your personal wound and be able to put it into words. A comforting thought, perhaps.

Read *Wounded Bud: Poems for Meditation by Alfred K. Lamotte*

Mercury/Uranus

Ideas bounce into the world. The mind goes on a joy ride—insights from on high. Ideas we have now tend to be excellent ones. Solutions to problems are more easily uncovered through thinking outside the box. Brainstorming is highlighted.

Read *Original Thinking: A Radical ReVisioning of Time, Humanity, and Nature by Glenn Aparicio Parry*

Mercury/Neptune

We may feel a little more confused. We are asked to trust our intuition. Our reasoning mind may be able to interpret the intuitive insights of this time with greater aptitude. Tune in to your inner voice and tune out the noise of the popular and distracting discourse.

Read *The Power of Myth by Joseph Campbell*

Mercury/Pluto

We can understand more of our current evolutionary journey. The trickster within may shed light on something we have been keeping secret—something we may have been keeping secret from ourselves, even.

Read Alchemy of Nine Dimensions: Decoding the Vertical Axis, Crop Circles, and the Mayan Calendar by Barbara Hand Clow

Mercury/Ascendant

We know what we want more clearly and communicate it with strength and truth. Clear speaking and revealing the truth enhance relationships.

Read *Oscar Wilde's Wit and Wisdom: A Book of Quotations by Oscar Wilde*

Mercury/Midheaven

This is a good transit for signing contracts and making decisions about our work or home lives.

Read *Clear your Clutter with Feng Shui by Karen Kingston*

~~~~~~~~~~

Stones for support in Mercury transit:
Mercury likes clarity of mind—use the **Agates** especially **Blue Lace Agate** for supporting clear thinking. I also like **Fluorite** for opening the mind and expanding what is possible. **Lapis Lazuli** is an excellent stone for speaking truth and opening our throat chakra. **Calcite** helps with concentration and focus. **Emerald** is considered a good stone for enhancing Mercury in our chart.

Venus Transits

Perceived Effect: Venus serves to assist us in opening our hearts to love, beauty and abundance. She invites us to live in the sensuous pleasures of being human. As we open our hearts and listen more deeply, Venus reveals the sacred intentions of our life on this beautiful globe. Living a creative life is about stepping into new ways of seeing the world, and these transits support us in doing exactly that.

Lessons: Venus teaches us about the pleasures of Earthly life. Venus wants us to experience this human life with joy, love and sensuality. Venus teaches us to enjoy life. She wants us to value art, beauty, creativity and the experiences of being human which go beyond survival. She wants us to fall in love, dance wildly at midnight and indulge our senses.

Retrograde: Venus goes retrograde for approximately 40 days every other year. It is the basis for the mystical wandering in the desert for 40 days and 40 nights. This is a wonderful time for going into our own inner creative process. Start with the first creative project that comes to mind and see where it takes you. Allow these weeks to be an opening into a relationship and creation that you have been yearning for, even if the longing has been entirely in secret.

Orbit: Venus takes 224.65 earth days to get around the Sun. It is the only planet where a day is longer than a year. It takes 242 earth days for Venus to rotate on its axis. The synodic cycle of the Earth and Venus (the time between conjunctions) is 584 days.

Orb: 3° (As with Mercury retrograde, when Venus transits a natal planet during the retrograde period, it is essentially transiting that planet for the entire duration of the retrograde plus 3° on either end.)

Time it takes: Normally, Venus takes four or five days to transit a point in the chart. If it retrogrades over a point, it could take up to four months and will be a very auspicious transit.

~~~~~~~~~~

Venus/Sun

Enjoy the simple pleasures of a sunny day—at least in our innards. Let passion reign. Open to love. Go on an artist's date with yourself.

Read *Pride and Prejudice by Jane Austen*

Venus/Moon

The passionate side of Venus enhances the emotionally receptive side of the Moon. Dancing, playing and creating are highlighted by this transit. Let emotions and feelings flow with the tides.

Read *Dream Work by Mary Oliver*

Venus/Mercury

Allow Venus to open up the creative side of your brain. Make time for imaginative conversations that take you into a more beautiful state of mind. Go visit a museum or art gallery. Read good literature.

Read *The Alchemist by Paolo Coehlo*

Venus/Venus

Venus-to-Venus transits tend to be quite lovely no matter how hard the aspect. There is more support right now for our creative endeavors. Open to love, both divine and human (if indeed there is any difference).

Read *Sonnets from the Portuguese: A Celebration of Love by Elizabeth Barrett Browning*

Venus/Mars

A passionate time where creative instincts are heightened, potential for new love increases and an old love gets a new boost. Stay conscious of what you are attracting and bringing into your current relationships. We may have a tendency to antagonize or instigate tension at this time. What we are really looking for is release. If sex isn't an option, do art in any of its myriad of forms.

Read *The Cosmic Embrace by John Stevens*

Venus/Jupiter

The desire nature gets a boost and our longing may intensify. While we may feel more buoyant and joyful we may also feel less grounded. Overindulgence is a handicap of these two getting together, while the ability to attract prosperity is the bonus.

Read *Creating True Prosperity by Shakti Gawain*

Venus/Nodes

Notice what happens in relationships at this time. We may have important soul mate connections, meet a soul mate or have an intimate connection that supports our soul work. This can also be a creative time, especially creativity that comes from the depths of our soul.

Read *Sacred Contracts by Carolyn Myss*

Venus/Saturn

We may find that love takes hold where often we feel restricted and stuck. The opportunity here is for forgiveness and the release of grudges, resentments and old patterns of negativity. The creativity of Venus supports the disciplined side of Saturn in opening to new artistic ventures. It is a good time to practice your craft.

Read *The Artist's Way by Julia Cameron*

Venus/Chiron

Where we feel wounded opens, the toxins release and we have the ability to heal again. These transits are also good transits for meeting a soul mate or beginning a significant relationship.

Read *Botanica Erotica: Arousing Body, Mind, and Spirit* by *Diana De Luca*

Venus/Uranus

Some creative insight into what makes us tick, change, and feel out of control at times. Use art to tune into forces that often feel outside of our sphere of influence.

Read *Love Poems from God: Twelve Sacred Voices from the East and West* by *Daniel Ladinsky*

Venus/Neptune

This is a chance to align our personal relationships with our spiritual paths. Open and feel the love. This is a time to pay attention to dreams, visions and creative openings. This is a lovely time to pick up a paintbrush, a quill or dance under the light of the Moon. This transit supports falling in love, but often like falling in love we may not know what is really going on until after the transit is over.

Read *Art as Medicine: Creating a Therapy of the Imagination* by *Shaun McNiff*

Venus/Pluto

This is a chance, through the expression of beauty and love, to understand why and how we came to be so bent on changing our life. Our desire for transformation pushes us to search for the truth in our relationships.

Read *A Return to Love by Marianne Williamson*

Venus/Ascendant

We may appear more attractive at this time. It is a good time for making changes to our appearance, for purchasing clothes or getting a haircut. While brief, it can also be a creative time.

Read *All About Love by Bell Hooks*

Venus/Midheaven

We may feel inspired to be more creative in our work and home life. This is a good time to redecorate or purchase furniture. We may make larger decisions about buying or selling a home at this time if other longer-term transits are present that are good for this as well.

Read *House Magic: The Good Witch's Guide to Bringing Grace to Your Space by Ariana*

~~~~~~~~~~

Stones for support in Venus transit:

Venus likes **Malachite** for getting in touch with our human sensual experience and power, and for helping with love-sickness. **Rose Quartz, Rhodonite** and **Rhodochrosite** are all good stones when dealing with relationship issues. Rhodochrosite, in particular, helps us to get at the deeper issues that are going on beneath the issue at hand. Rose quartz tends to be soothing. **Jade** is another Venus stone, supportive of magnetizing love and sustaining relationship and fortune. **Pink Tourmaline** is supportive of the heart chakra. **Diamond** is the stone to maximize Venus' effect.

Mars Transits

Perceived Effect: Mars appears to support the use of will or blocks the use of power. It does not rule the power itself but *how* the power is used. Things can "heat up" during a Mars transit. It is a planet that instigates and moves energy.

Lessons: Mars teaches us that we have a will. It is through Mars that we desire to be human and come into this Life. Mars teaches us how to direct ourselves, how to behave,

67

how to initiate and how to attack. Mars teaches us that we are in control of our lives and our actions. Mars is easily a trigger planet, especially for Pluto and Uranus transits.

Retrograde: Mars goes retrograde for approximately three months every two years. Its retrograde periods are important to note since they come on strong and stay for a while. Mars rules our will and desire to act.

Potentially, Mars retrograde periods can help us to alter the way we experience our aggressive energy and the way we do war on this planet. It is a powerful time to work with the third chakra and the root chakra—both Mars centers. With Mars retrograde, a shift may occur internally at first. It is an extraordinary time to look at how we are violent with ourselves and with others either through words, thoughts, physically or psychically. Mars, the god of war, was the instigator and motivator for many a drive or battle. Mars in our natal chart is about how we motivate and drive ourselves. What gets us up in the morning? What motivates us to succeed? To be kind? To change the world? During this time, we may feel motivated from a new source—perhaps a source of love and compassion.

Orbit: The Synodic cycle of Mars lasts for 780 earth days. Mars goes retrograde for about 72 days every other year. A Mars year is about 1.88 Earth years. Interestingly, Mars is very close in size to the Earth. It is also tilted at 25°, which is very close to the Earth's 23° tilt, and its day is also about the same length as an Earth day at 24 hours 39 minutes.

Orb: 3° As with Venus and Mercury retrograde periods,

the transit lasts for the entire retrograde period. When Mars transits a natal planet during the retrograde period, it is essentially transiting that planet for the entire duration of the retrograde plus 3° on either end

Time it takes: If Mars is simply moving direct over a natal planet, this transit takes about a week. If it retrogrades over a natal planet, then it could last up to seven months and those will be a very powerful, transformational seven months.

~~~~~~~~~~

Mars/Sun

Mars triggers the life-giving solar rays to emanate more strongly and with greater intensity. Wear a hat and sunscreen and enjoy the added energy.

Read *Body Thrive: Uplevel Your Body and Your Life with 10 Habits from Ayurveda and Yoga by Cate Stillman*

Mars/Moon

Mars triggers the emotional, receptive side of lunar energy allowing for the possibility of greater intensity of feeling, especially any feelings we have repressed—joy, anger, and grief.

Read *Fire in the Earth by David Whyte*

Mars/Mercury

Mars instigates the mind to take over and we have the opportunity to figure things out, communicate with gusto and initiate discussion. Becoming overly mental or rational is a potential side effect. Use this time to organize and clear clutter. Mars supports Mercury to actively gain clarity through cleaning and working hard.

Read *The Life-Changing Art of Tidying Up: The Japanese Art of Decluttering and Organizing by Marie Kondo*

Mars/Venus

Mars dancing with Venus enlivens our passionate, sexual nature. Our creative and artistic side also gets a boost. Perhaps a greater degree of focus on relationships also occurs with this transit. Mars wants us to take a risk—so take a risk for love. Take a risk to put forth a work of art.

Read *Finding God Through Sex: Awakening the One of Spirit Through the Two of Flesh by David Deida*

Mars/Mars

While agitation and frustration may be one of the side effects of this transit, we are being asked by Mars to find our will to live, our will to act and our will to be in truth. Taking a stand for our truth may be very important at this time and will likely meet with a better outcome if we take six deep breaths before jumping off any proverbial cliffs.

Read *Emergent Strategy: Shaping Change, Changing Worlds by Adrienne Maree Brown*

Mars/Jupiter

Mars instigates Jupiter to expand in the area involved (house and sign). We may feel more assertive to inspire growth and hope. Watch for the sudden appearance of an opportunity.

Read *The Pursuit of Happiness: Integrating the Chakras for Complete Harmony by David Pond*

Mars/Nodes

Mars activates and triggers a desire and a response. When Mars transits the Nodes, it pushes us to make changes and to take action in response to an impulse. We may feel an added push in a direction that doesn't necessarily make sense. This is a good time to follow gut instincts.

Read *Altars of Power and Grace: Create the Life You Desire by Robin and Michael Mastro*

Mars/Saturn

We may feel more ambitious, more driven and at the same time more blocked and more limited. Mars triggers the point in our chart where we have the most to learn. Being able to be humble, honest and patient with ourselves will help the most during this transit. A daily practice supports us in working towards a goal.

Read *Outliers by Malcolm Gladwell*

Mars/Chiron

An old wound is lanced. We want intensely to heal and get to the bottom of a present hurt. A crisis may help us clear out negativity or clear a block to creativity.

Read *Chiron: The Rainbow Bridge Between the Inner & Outer Planets by Barbara Hand Clow*

Mars/Uranus

A potent, if short, transit that offers the possibility for change, happy accidents, synchronicities, and generally being out of control. Long for the excitement and joy of these changes.

Read *The Spontaneous Fulfillment of Desire: Harnessing the*

Infinite Power of Coincidence by Deepak Chopra

Mars/Neptune

Here is the potential for a sudden overwhelming drive to know God, to dive deep into our spiritual nature and to know our true purpose. We may want to delve deeper into the truth of our relationships and initiate a process that brings greater intimacy in our lives. Trust the process. Trust life. Everything is flowing in perfection.

Read *Their Eyes Were Watching God by Zora Neale Hurston*

Mars/Pluto

With this transit, we are offered the chance to take a turn in the spiral of fate of our lives. We can change direction and more adequately align with our soul's intention and growth. It is here when the desire for power meets the experience of power.

Read *Transcending the Global Power Game: Hidden Agendas, Divine Intervention and the New Earth by Armin Risi*

Mars/Ascendant

We may have added strength and power at this time. It is a good time for competition, sports or physical exercise. At the same time we can easily overtax ourselves or feel more frustrated. Pay attention to what you really need and pursue that. Take extra time if you are feeling added agitation. This will pass.

Read *The Art of War by Sun Tzu Translated by Thomas Cleary*

Mars/Midheaven

Pay attention to avoid making rash decisions. Take an extra breath before making changes. We may have added courage to take risks at this time. If the longer-term transits are good for making changes, use this transit to take a leap forward. If the longer transits are challenging, take extra time with your decision and wait until this passes to be sure you are on the highest track for your soul.

Read *The Re-Enchantment of Everyday Life by Thomas Moore*

~~~~~~~~~~

Stones for a challenging Mars transit:

The effects of a challenging Mars transit can be frustration and rage—either the Mars energy is very intense and we are blocking it or the Mars energy is being diverted through muscles that have not been used in a while. If we are feeling overly frustrated due to blocking the energy, **Carnelian** supports us in feeling more courage. This stone helps us deal with our frustrations and fears that are often triggered during Mars transits. Sometimes, as when Mars is in a water sign, we may resonate with **Tiger's Eye** that helps us to focus when we have a lot of energy but do not know how to use it. **Amazonite** is an excellent stone for aligning our will with a higher will and channeling information needed to guide our next steps.

Jupiter Transits

Perceived Effect: Jupiter serves to expand whatever it is transiting. Jupiter wants things to be so large that we *have* to deal with them. It is hard to ignore Jupiter's transit, since for better or worse it lets us know what is going on.

Lessons: Jupiter teaches us that everything can be seen, at least by someone. Nothing is hidden with Jupiter. Jupiter tells us that everything and anything is possible. It is the planet of endless possibilities. It wants us to experience the fullness of the joy of life. Any place and in any way that we block joy becomes apparent and exacerbated during a Jupiter transit. We are asked to open and accept our own Great Nature.

The dark side of Jupiter is a tendency to over-indulge, to exaggerate, to be extravagant, and to overdo a good thing. Our current culture here in America is like a Jupiter retrograde culture. It seems like the more we have, the more we want. That is the dark side of Jupiter.

Retrograde: With Jupiter retrograde, the desire to expand and the propensity of life to get bigger takes a back seat and we can take some time to ground, contract, get clear, get sober and face the facts of life. Thank goodness for Jupiter—but who would want to live like that all the time? During Jupiter retrograde, we can feel the relief of grounded-ness if there has been too much expansion in our life.

Orbit: Jupiter's cycle around the Earth takes between 11 and 12 years. It takes about one year to move through a sign (this varies greatly depending on retrograde periods).
Orb: 3°
Time it takes: Jupiter transits a point in the chart either once or three times. If Jupiter transits a planet three times, then the transit begins when Jupiter gets within 3° of the

natal point in its approach. The transit lasts until Jupiter gets 3° past the exact point after the last transit. This means that between the first and last transits of Jupiter, the orb may be greater (and often is) than 3°. During those in-between times when Jupiter may be as far away as 10°, and we know it's going to be exact again, the transit is still, noticeably occurring, but without full intensity. However, if Jupiter is 10° away, the effect may be noticeably less significant unless there is a major trigger, like a Mars conjunction at the same time. Multiple transits crossing the same planet increase the likelihood of events of the nature of the transit to happen.

Time it takes: It depends on whether Jupiter retrogrades back over the natal planet. If it does not retrograde over the planet or point, this transit can be as short as a month. If it does retrograde over the planet or point, it could last up to ten months.

~~~~~~~~~~~

Jupiter/Sun

Open to the big world around you. The Sun wants to come out. During this time we open to new possibilities that enhance our state of beingness. The world sees us better and bigger than before. We can expand our worlds to include greater prosperity and enjoyment.

Read *Open Secret: Versions of Rumi by John Moyne and Coleman Barks*

Jupiter/Moon

We may feel intensely and openly emotional. We may feel out of control with our emotions or as if our feelings have a life of their own. Our mothers or our issues with our mothers may show up more. Some areas or issues in our lives that have been difficult to understand, see or access can become available at this time for greater awareness.

Read *Women Who Run with the Wolves by Clarissa Pinkola Estes*

Jupiter/Mercury

This is an excellent transit for the mind. Lots of thinking. Lots of ideas. Lots of brainstorming or whatever it is that your brain likes to partake in. If you tend to be a logical thinker, then your ability to reason expands. If you tend to think out of the box, this is a wonderful time for new ideas. Writing, publishing, speaking, orating, political work, and philosophical understanding are all highlighted. We can have a major insight or breakthrough into the work of our life.

Read *The Biology of Belief by Bruce H. Lipton Ph. D.*

Jupiter/Venus

Here is the opportunity to fall in love, if we dare. If we don't, overindulgence is an easy way to suppress any feelings of possibility. We may feel more inspired to be creative. It is time to open to sensual pleasure and the joy of inspired creativity.

Read *Anna Karenina by Leo Tolstoy*

Jupiter/Mars

This may be a difficult transit to contain. We may tend to be more impulsive, more aggressive or more frustrated. On another level, there is an opportunity for taking action and asserting ourselves in the direction we choose.

Read *The Lord of the Rings by J.R.R. Tolkien*

Jupiter/Jupiter

This is a time when we are learning how to create opportunities in the world. Jupiter is a planet that connects to society, culture, education and reasoning. Jupiter challenges us to find our path and make a difference in the world. Jupiter wishes for us to experience true prosperity, excitement and choice. With Jupiter we have options. We create our reality and we enjoy or feel overwhelmed by our creation. This cycle is a cycle of opportunities in the world. During our first Jupiter return, which happens when Jupiter conjuncts itself around the age of twelve, we set forth to find that the world is a good place filled with hope and possibility. It is a time to have positive experiences of what can be done and to know that we are given permission to try new things, make mistakes without judgment and learn through curiosity and a true desire to understand life. If hard knocks come during our first Jupiter return, we often develop a pattern of looking at the glass as half empty. Each subsequent Jupiter return is a chance to find out differently—that world is full of possibility.

Read *Creating Affluence by Deepak Chopra*

Jupiter/Nodes

This is a very auspicious transit for meeting a significant teacher, soul mate or wise person. What we learn during this time is important for our soul growth, especially when Jupiter conjuncts the North Node. When Jupiter conjuncts the South Node, it supports bringing in gifts from past lives. Open to what comes through.

Read *The Kabir Book: Forty-Four of the Ecstatic Poems of Kabir, Versions by Robert Bly*

Jupiter/Saturn

This transit sheds light on how we limit ourselves and shows us a doorway out of our own self-imposed confinement. Or we may feel even more confined. The feeling of being limited, controlled or punished may show up in order to push us to find the way out of those experiences.

Read *To the Lighthouse by Virginia Woolf*

Jupiter/Chiron

Now is an opportunity to heal our core wound. The wound becomes increasingly visible and more significantly encountered and experienced in order that we glean insight into the healing that is necessary.

Read *The Fifth Sacred Thing by Starhawk*

Jupiter/Uranus

The degree to which we feel out of control or are afraid of being out of control of our lives is the degree to which Jupiter will enhance and accelerate the deliverance of any sense we have that there is such a thing as control. Look for understanding of the nature of intuition, synchronicity and the possibility that all change is interrelated—*and* that we have influence over all change yet control over none.

Read *The Big Leap: Conquer Your Hidden Fear and Take Life to the Next Level by Gay Hendricks, M.D.*

Jupiter/Neptune

Jupiter represents our belief systems—religions, dogmas, and spiritual concepts. Neptune represents the psychic realm—our connection with spirit, raw and true, our ability to tap into realms unseen, and our trust in the process of Life. Neptune demands trust and letting go. We swim through the sea of unknowing. Jupiter calls to us to make sense of Life, asks us to project our thoughts and understandings into the world. Jupiter asks us to "understand" what we know intuitively from Neptune. With these two planets in transit we are dealing in full light with any conflicts between our belief systems and intuition—our psychic knowing. This is the inherent conflict between "conceptual understanding" and "knowing".

Read *The Teachings of Don Juan: A Yaqui Way of Knowledge by Carlos Castenada*

Jupiter/Pluto

With these two colliding, we are taught the nature of transformation—not just change, but complete alchemical transmutation of form. The material world that often seems so settled, dense, immutable, and constant changes form before our eyes. The possibility of deep change, the potential for the door to be opened to our deepest, darkest fears, secrets, and gifts is opened by the ever-giving light of Jupiter. Great opportunities for a new life emerge if we can let go beyond fear.

Read *Pluto: The Evolutionary Journey of the Soul* by *Jeff Green*

Jupiter/Ascendant

When Jupiter conjuncts the Ascendant, we begin a twelve-year cycle of growth and openings. Jupiter opens doors and shows us our highest direction. When Jupiter crosses the Ascendant we see our purpose more clearly. When it crosses the Descendant, we open to what we want in relationship.

Read *The Wisdom of Insecurity* by *Alan Watts*

Jupiter/Midheaven

When Jupiter conjuncts the MC, work opportunities open up for us and we can make a job change. I rarely see people go unemployed during this transit.

When Jupiter conjuncts the Imum Coeli, we may decide to move or find a great new place to live. At the very least, we usually get the longing for a new home or change in our environment. The next year is a good time to move; so open to it if that is something you want.

When Jupiter squares the Midheaven or IC, it is usually also conjunct the Ascendant or Descendant.

Read *Liberating Your Magnificence: Opening Your Life to Infinite Possibilities* by *Shannon Peck and Scott Peck*

~~~~~~~~~~~

Stones for a challenging Jupiter transit:
Jupiter wants expansion and growth-wants us to experience more, learn more and do more. Yet the challenge of a difficult Jupiter transit can be desire—too much desire—too much "the grass-is-always-greener", too much yearning for something we do not have. Stones that help us accept life as it is are good for this challenge. **Calcite** and **Onyx** are good stones for that. **Lapis Lazuli** can be a good stone for a Jupiter transit in that it helps us see and speak truth—rather than pie-in-the-sky fantasies of what may be possible in the future. **Topaz** and **Citrine** are Jupiter's stones for enhancing and bringing forth Jupiter in a more potent way.

Jupiter through the Houses

Jupiter takes twelve years to move through the houses. It lives in each house for a year.

Jupiter in the 1st House
We have the chance to open to a new sense of ourselves. We get a new lease on life. It is a good time to change our appearance in support and harmony with this new cycle.

Jupiter in the 2nd House
This is a time when we are open to abundance. It is a year

of greater ease in our physical worlds, when resources become more available to us.

Jupiter in the 3rd House
This is a powerful year for study and for understanding new concepts. It is a good year for taking road trips or short journeys that help us see the world with new eyes.

Jupiter in the 4th House
This is often a year when we move—as we open ourselves to having the home space that we desire. This is also an excellent year to spend time with family or to begin a family of our own. Jupiter in the 4th is a transit that supports conception and also the transition out of these temporary bodies.

Jupiter in the 5th House
Jupiter in the 5th house opens us to our full creative potential. This is a great year to focus on our art. It is also an easier time to have children and/or a year when we can enjoy the presence and company of our children. We may have a longing for children during this time that we hadn't had before this time.

Jupiter in the 6th House
Jupiter likes expansion and Jupiter in the house of health may present some health challenges. Expansion and growth can be challenging for our bodies. Underlying health conditions may appear larger. The magnifying glass offers us a chance to heal a condition that may have been lying dormant, but needed our attention. Focus on new

health habits. A lifestyle change can open us to new opportunities. We may feel a bit ungrounded and spacy during this year. What new routines will help you grow?

Jupiter in the 7th House

This is a time when our relationships may seem too small for us, or too confining. We want growth in our lovers and in our experience in the world. We want our relationships to get better. Sometimes we become dissatisfied with our relationship, while the grass is greener elsewhere. This can also be a year of opening to new relationship, especially if we are single. Also, our careers can find new opportunities for expansion and growth.

Jupiter in the 8th House

This is a great year for diving into research, for studying the mysteries of life. It is also an indication of a possible inheritance. Money from others expands and we are more open to receiving wealth and prosperity.

Jupiter in the 9th House

This is a wonderful year for travel and for higher study. Jupiter likes the 9th House and we can open to adventure and journeys that bring us closer to our highest purpose.

Jupiter in the 10th House

This is often a time when career opportunities present themselves. I look at the house Saturn is in to consider at what stage and level these possibilities will operate. Often we get job offers during this time, even if we weren't looking. This is a good year for promotions as well.

Jupiter in the 11th House

We can be recognized and rewarded for our work at this time. Our circle of friends expands and we may find a tribe, organization or other kind of group that supports us on our spiritual journey.

Jupiter in the 12th House

This is a chance to study the deeper mysteries in life. We are asked to trust our intuition and step into divine guidance. Spending time alone in retreat is beneficial during this time.

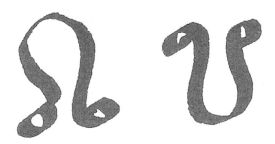

The Moon's Nodes

Perceived Effect: Fated events that disrupt our life so that we recognize the deeper patterns that we live by. Nodal transits point out our "stuff". They show us our deep soul issues and gifts, places where growth is needed. The Nodal transits upset our habitual stance in the world.

Lessons: Nodal transits come along to bring out our deepest soul desires. These desires often erupt in us to help us clear past life conditioning. Soul work often has a life of its own. It can be hard to logically understand what is going on within us and around us during these times.

Little things can take on greater significance and we can glide through this transit with greater ease if we pay attention to the signs that occur in the little stuff. There are hidden signs in everything that point us toward our truest soul direction. These times can be times of upheaval and radical life changes. We are often challenged to look at our lives under a microscope. What isn't in true alignment needs to change. Often we meet significant people during these times, people who change our lives. They tend to impact us and change the course we are on. Since the Nodes are the underlying tone for eclipses, we experience Nodal transits as disruptive and upsetting.

Retrograde*:* The Nodes move in a retrograde direction in general. In my observation, there is little difference between the retrograde and direct motion of the Nodes. What is more significant is where the Eclipses land. (See the section below under orb.)

Orbit: 18.6 years. The Nodes move backward through the Zodiac.

Orb*:* To time the greatest impact of a Lunar Nodal transit, we must take note of the eclipses. An eclipse occurs when the Sun, Moon and Earth align with the Lunar Nodes. Eclipses occur at the New and Full moons and can be aligned with either the South Node or the North Node.

For the most significant nodal transits, note when an eclipse conjuncts or opposes your lunar nodes, Sun, Moon, or Ascendant. The transit is in effect from the time of the eclipse through the next six months. Pay attention to other planets triggering that particular point.

For example: If your Sun is at 9° Virgo and a Solar Eclipse occurs at 10° Virgo in September, then the transit will last from September until the following March—or until the next series of eclipses which will be in February or March. If Saturn moves through 10° Sagittarius, that will be a trigger. Or Mars moves through 10° Pisces, the opposite point, that would also be a trigger.

When the nodes square, trine or sextile a planet or point in your chart, the effects are much less noticeable, yet can still be experienced.

Time it takes: Either two or three eclipse seasons, either one year or one and a half years.

~~~~~~~~~~~

Nodes/Sun

The disruption points to where we are being overly egotistical and proud. This transit is designed to take us down a notch so that we can receive the beauty of this life with humility.

Read *Astrology for the Soul by Jan Spillman*

Nodes/Moon

This transit shows us our blind spots and upsets us into experiencing our emotions more fully so that we can grow into greater compassion with awareness.

Read *The Red Tent by Anita Diamant*

Nodes/Mercury

This is often a disruption in our financial situation. Finances are all about what we value. This transit asks us to change our values so that they are more in alignment with our true purpose.

Read *Walden by Henry David Thoreau*

Nodes/Venus

The disruption is in our love lives. How we love gets called into question so that we can open to a greater love.

Read *The Prophet by Kahlil Gibran*

Nodes/Mars

While Mars rarely allows us the chance to fall into a rut, we may over use willpower and guts when allowance and acceptance are more appropriate for the moment. Nodal transits to Mars teach us that there is a force greater than our personal will. Our true happiness during this transit comes from aligning our personal will with divine will or a higher power. In this transit we learn to surrender to the forces of fate.

Read *The Celestine Prophecy by James Redfield*

Nodes/Jupiter

When the Nodes transit Jupiter we are challenged to expand our vision and broaden our horizons. We need to open to new possibilities. In typical Nodal fashion, the opening occurs because something in our life doesn't go our way. Something better comes in when we let go of having to have it happen "our way". Release control and see what happens.

Read *Energy Strands: The Ultimate Guide to Clearing the Cords That Are Constricting Your Life by Denise Linn*

Nodes/Nodes

These transits teach us more about our soul patterns—the cellular memories that have been passed down through other lives and through our ancestors. Important teachers come into our life at this time to point out a course correction. Pay attention.

Read *Care of the Soul by Thomas Moore*

Nodes/Saturn

When the Nodes transit our natal Saturn, we must change something that has been stuck deep in our psyches. We have to look at a harsh reality. The disruption pushes us to break through blockages and let go of something very old that we have been holding onto. Particularly in our work lives, we have to deal with the reality that is being presented and make a different choice.

Read *Healing the Shame that Binds You by John Bradshaw*

Nodes/Chiron

The disruption at this time wakes up an old wound in order to support healing. Sometimes we need to dive back into an old issue to get at the roots of a current problem. Long-standing issues around relationship get triggered so that we can open to a truer love either in a current relationship or in a new, more truly loving one.

Read *The Way of the Shaman by Michael Harner*

Nodes/Uranus

When the Nodes transit Uranus, there is an underlying ripple in how we deal with change. Events may seem out of our hands. Changes that seem small on the outside, feel big on the inside.

Read *Soul Retrieval: Mending the Fragmented Self through Shamanic Practice* by Sandra Ingerman

Nodes/Neptune

This is a very disorienting transit since what is going on may have very little validation in our everyday lives. The spiritual shift appears in our dreams and fantasies. We may start longing for a different life. We may need to wait for other transits to bring things into form. For now, patience and deepening into our spiritual practice can have profound results.

Read *Conversations with God: An Uncommon Dialogue* by Neale Donald Walsch

Nodes/Pluto

The Nodes offer us opportunities to become more empowered. The changes at this time push us to know ourselves. We may be challenged to adjust to larger events happening in the world, pushing us to find our avenue of power in changing the world. There may be a loss at this time, a loss that shows us the truth.

Read *Shakespeare, anything by Shakespeare*

Nodes/Ascendant

This is an important time to evaluate our priorities. We can become aware of long-term issues that have been running our lives, soul issues, and ancestral patterns. We may find that we are confronted to deal with something unpleasant that we have been avoiding. Healing sessions at this time can be very powerful. If we open to embrace the truth of who we are, we can open to a new way of being free from an old pattern that no longer serves us.

Read *The Diamond in Your Pocket: Discovering Your True Radiance by Gangaji and Eckhart Tolle*

Nodes/Midheaven

The work of finding our calling can easily open to some of us, if we are called on a path that is well worn or straightforward. For most of us, we will have twists and turns on a journey to find a path that is authentic to our soul. This transit supports the work of aligning our soul work with our path of service. We may also be working out issues with our family and home life. Where we live may be called into question. It may be time to find a place to live that calls to us more truly.

Read *Grist for the Mill by Ram Daas*

~~~~~~~~~~~

Stones for a challenging Nodal transit:
Onyx supports protection if there is turbulence during this transit. **Agate** and **Hessonite** are the stones of the North Node. **Tiger's Eye** and **Turquoise** are good stones for the South Node.

Saturn Transits

Perceived Effect: Saturn in transit challenges us to take responsibility for our decisions, issues and actions in the world. We are forced to look at how we block our full and joyous expression in the world. Saturn demands that we deal with issues that have been holding us back. Sometimes, in light of having our challenges shoved in our face, we feel depressed and tired. Saturn is a planet of pressure and contraction. It is natural in a Saturn transit to feel de-pressed, like we are being pushed into a smaller container than what we need to live. Saturn in truth is asking us to grow—but the growth must come through having the utmost of integrity. In general, Saturn transits go best when we accept the conditions of our current situation no matter how wonderful or difficult they appear. Trying to escape tends to make our lives more difficult.

Lessons: Our experiences in life, our genes, our moment of birth, our ancestors and their traditions and many other things—along with our past prior to this life—all work together to create our *perspective*. Our perspective creates our reality along with co-creating everyone else's reality. There are places and ways we have learned to block reality—the luminous perfect reality of bliss. Our vision is blocked. Saturn is the planet that teaches us how we are shutting down to Life. Its lessons are not always pleasant. Sometimes there is sorrow and loss. If we are experiencing sorrow and loss during this time, then we are tuned into Saturn and have a chance of transforming an old blockage. Be open to the possibility of true transformation and joy even in the midst of hardship.

Seriousness is called for with Saturn. Clear boundaries, conscious intent, perseverance and restraint are the lessons. We can set our minds to what we have to do and accomplish what has felt insurmountable before. Saturn supports us in being strong-willed, cautious and determined. Take advantage of this time to do hard work. If you feel stuck, depressed or scared, pick a project you have wanted to get to—like cleaning out a closet, or organizing files—and get to work.

Retrograde: With Saturn retrograde, we are in recovery, recuperation, re-membering, re-living, re-organizing and re-structuring.

Orbit: Saturn takes 29.7 years to get around the Sun and thus the Earth.

Orb: 3° As with other planets, this orb applies to the approach and release of the transit. The transit is in effect during the entire retrograde period that includes the transit of the planet. I will often notice a significant decrease in the effect of Saturn within one degree after the last time it transits the natal planet.

Time it takes: One year—with the exception of Saturn conjunct the Moon and the Saturn return. When Saturn conjuncts the Moon, I use a seven year time period corresponding to the Vedic "Sade Sati", which uses a 45-degree orb. The Saturn return is felt strongly the year before it is exact, sometimes even two years before being exact.

~~~~~~~~~~~

Saturn/Sun

Our very radiance and life force depends on us accepting the work at hand. This can be a wonderful time if we pare down, cut back, say no to extras, create a plan and focus on what *needs* to get done. Let go of materialistic desires and take care of the needs at hand. When we do, we may find that the hard work of the moment becomes enjoyable and deeply rewarding. Simplicity is key. The simple joy of doing the necessary work fills our heart. Often during this transit we feel down, depressed and low energy. Watch how saying "No" can lift your spirits. Giving ourselves permission to do less and feel more is one of the great antidotes for this transit.

Read *The Four Agreements: A Practical Guide to Personal Freedom (A Toltec Wisdom Book) by Don Miquel Ruiz*

Saturn/Moon

This is a time to look into emotional issues that have been blocking our hearts from opening. Take this year to practice unblocking emotionally. Responsibilities for family and home may increase. Like all Saturn transits, it is helpful to look at what is needed and let the wants go. Another time when Saturn's mal-effect can express as depression. Yet, there are many new theories about depression and its possible healing potential in and of itself. Perhaps the feeling of depression is a call to slow down. Saturn likes us to move slowly and steadily. Work methodically and with integrity. Definitely say no when possible. When we don't know what to do, do nothing—sit still and wait. Let the mood change. Less is more.

Read *The Year of Magical Thinking by Joan Didion*

Saturn conjuncts the Moon: The Sade Sati

When transiting Saturn joins our natal Moon it has special significance in Vedic astrology. It is known as a particularly challenging time. It lasts for about seven years* and comes around every 21 years. In general, take the year Saturn conjuncts the Moon and add three years on either side. This is the time frame when familial responsibilities weigh heavier. It is often a time of loss. Dennis Flaherty likens this transit to winter—when the energy of the season goes into the roots. We don't always see the growth that is occurring, but it is significant and important.

   * Use a 45° orb

Saturn/Mercury

With this transit we can think with greater clarity and feel more certain of ourselves. The challenge is to stay open to the fact that we are not always "right". There is infinity of "right" perspectives. This can be a good time to plan, set goals, sign contracts and do legal activities. While the process may go slowly, it moves with certainty and logic. Mercury rules commerce and how we place value on the stuff of life. When Saturn transits Mercury, it gives us the opportunity to reflect on our values and change what is not true for us.

   Read *Sacred Economics: Money, Gift & Society in the Age of Transition by Charles Eisenstein*

Saturn/Venus

In the case that our natal Venus offers us wild rides of the imagination, Saturn may have a sobering effect. In the case that we are blocked to our creative impulses, Saturn may give us a good push toward discovering our inner artist in whatever form they appear.

   Read *The Law of Attraction: The Basics of the Teachings of Abraham by Esther and Jerry Hicks*

Saturn/Mars

If our will is strong, Saturn may show us how the "larger" will governs all. If our will is weak, Saturn may give us a nudge towards strengthening this important energy center.

It seems that we can trust Saturn to teach us exactly what we need to learn. When it aspects Mars, whatever we desire shows up either as the thing to get rid of or the thing to go for. Usually the signs are clear. Hard work and physical exercise is a good antidote to the feeling that life is difficult.

Read *Chop Wood, Carry Water: A Guide to Finding Fulfillment in Everyday Life by Rick Fields and Peggy Taylor*

Saturn/Jupiter
Wherever we think we have it going on, the area of life where things move the smoothest, the place in us where we think we have it down—Saturn comes along to rock the boat. We all have ways in which we have figured out how to survive—a formula that helps us win, enjoy life and which seems to work most of the time. Well, not right now. Now we need to look at some basic assumptions we have made about life and re-work these.

Read *Think and Grow Rich by Napoleon Hill*

Saturn/Nodes
When Saturn joins the South Node, we are in an important time of completing past-life patterns. We may get closure with a relationship or personal issue at this time. This is an important transit for letting go. When Saturn joins the North Node, we are asked to take responsibility for our soul work, to say yes to what is being asked of us. Often there is clarity about our particular calling in this world. We may experience pressure to move forward with our soul calling. Soul work often feels like it has a life of its own, something that may haunt us until we know it clearly.

This is a good transit for having that clarity. When Saturn squares the Nodes, we are challenged to pay more attention to our soul work. We may be confronted with long-term deep issues, blocks on our path. Feelings of insecurity or shame may arise as we get to the roots of past-life conditioning. It is important to pay attention to the messages that we receive at this time, even if we don't like the presentation.

Read *The Essential Sri Anandamayi Ma: Life and Teaching of a 20th Century Indian Saint by Anandamayi Ma and Joseph A. Fitzgerald*

Saturn/Saturn

Saturn-to-Saturn transits are very important times and often accompany significant changes in our lives. Saturn in our chart is a major player in looking at our relationship to our world, culture and society. Saturn shows us how to "deal" with life and the structures around us that we are co-creating with others. Saturn teaches us about boundaries. When Saturn transits itself, we are pointed in the direction of our true purpose. We learn where we hold ourselves back or push too hard. We are shown where and how we need to step up to the plate and be counted as an active, contributing and important member of this world. Seven-year cycles are often observed as important—the seven-year itch in relationships and seven-year stages in the development of humans. The seven-year cycle that corresponds to challenging aspects of Saturn to itself are times when issues of security, purpose, life direction, commitments, and responsibilities come up with greater intensity and often force a decision.

When Saturn conjuncts itself, it is called the Saturn return. This is a significant time in a person's life. It occurs between the ages of 27 and 30 and then again between 55 and 60 and then again between the ages of 84 and 87. During this time major life decisions come into question.

During the first Saturn return, there is a profound realization that we will die someday. No longer are we the immortal youth. We are called to take responsibility for what we are here to do, what we have come into this body for—our purpose. Now is a moment of decision making and following our path. Something must change. The karmic chords that bind us to our parents are broken and we are set free of their dreams and ideals for us. We can more easily see our own way in the world as a separate individual soul.

The second Saturn return is a sobering time of realizing that death is closer than we thought. With this comes a serious evaluation of our past. How have we lived? What has been important? What is left undone? Now we must evaluate what our priorities are. We are no longer beholden to the world in the same way, but are now beholden to spirit, and to bring in the spirit world for others. Usually there arises a deep sense that what the world thinks of us and expects from us no longer matters and with this realization comes a more profound experience of freedom.

Read *Zen and the Art of Motorcycle Maintenance by Robert M. Pirsig*

Saturn/Chiron

In the case that we did not know what our wound in life was, now we get an added boost towards greater understanding and compassion towards this important part of us. Saturn calls us to care for our wounds, enjoy our mistakes, love our humanness, and relish in the everydayness of life on this planet.

Read *Wherever You Go, There You Are: Mindfulness Meditation in Everyday-Life by Jon Kabat-Zinn*

Saturn/Uranus

Saturn is teaching us how to use our Uranian energy—how to feel vibration and know truth when we feel it in our bodies. This transit supports us in grounding our eccentricities into our real lives. Whatever makes us unusual needs to be accepted and taken seriously at this moment.

Read *Holy Here Wholy You: Discovering Your Authentic Self by Kim Lincoln*

Saturn/Neptune

At this time we are encouraged to ground our visions—make what we are most longing for real in our world. We are encouraged to take steps on our spiritual path, develop a spiritual practice and honor our dreams as real.

Read *Saturn: A New Look at an Old Devil by Liz Greene*

Saturn/Pluto

We are now challenged to align the actual circumstances in our lives with the deep transformation that we are longing for. Pluto in our natal chart is where we align with the evolution that is occurring within our generation and the transformation our generation is called to create. During this transit we must accept responsibility for being born when we were born and being part of the evolution of our planet and life form. We need to accept our age, our stage in life and our power to make a difference.

Read *Cosmos and Psyche: Intimations of a New World View by Richard Tarnas*

Saturn/Ascendant

Saturn always has a lesson to teach us. When it aligns with the Ascendant it teaches us to align how we present ourselves with what is in our heart and soul. We may get challenged to walk our talk. Others may challenge us to "get real" and we may have to get really honest with ourselves. When Saturn joins the Ascendant, we are beginning a new vocational cycle. We can get insights into our path, meet people who set a series of events in motion that lead to success, start a new job or school or some new career path. When Saturn crosses the Descendant, we are pulled more into the world, to bring our work to another level of success, to share our gifts with others and take responsibility for our unique calling.

Read *The Great Work of Your Life by Stephen Cope*

Saturn/Midheaven

Saturn conjunct the MC and IC are turning points in our lives. Saturn on the IC is a turning inward to focus on the roots of our work. It is time to focus on our foundation, our home life and what we want to build our career on. Time to take care of internal structures. When Saturn crosses the MC, we are supported in accepting full responsibility for our work. We may feel added pressure to step it up. We may be given extra work and responsibility.

Read *The Call by David Spangler*

~~~~~~~~~~

Stones for a challenging Saturn transit:
Saturn shows us where the walls are so that we can find the doors. Saturn wants us to make clear decisions and face up to our problems no matter what they are. If we are experiencing depression, lethargy or blockage, use **Topaz** for experiencing more joy and hope and **Turquoise** for vision. **Calcite** is an excellent stone in a Saturn transit since it supports clear decisions. **Onyx**, **Jet** and **Hematite** are also good stones since they help protect our energy fields and focus when we are feeling internal and external pressure. **Fluorite** is an excellent stone when we are feeling stuck and without vision—it helps us to open our mind and feel empowered to make changes in our lives. In Vedic astrology, the stone for Saturn is **Blue Sapphire**. Blue sapphire will accentuate Saturn's properties in your chart. If Saturn is a good planet for you and you want to build on this, blue sapphire is a good stone for you.

Saturn through the Houses

Saturn as it moves through houses marks the timing of our vocation/calling/career. It is an important cycle to pay attention to as a foundation for every other transit.

THE WHIRLING DANCE OF PLANETS

Saturn in 1st House
When Saturn crosses the Ascendant it begins a new cycle.
While Saturn is in the 1st house, we are finding ourselves
again. We are recreating ourselves. We are rebirthing into a
new identity.

Saturn in the 2nd House
We are defining and deciding what we really want in life.
Saturn pushes us, often through an experience of lack, to
truly recognize the life that we want.

Saturn in the 3rd House
Opportunities begin to open like popcorn. We may find
ourselves overwhelmed with the random offerings of this
time. Explore with great curiosity. This is a good time for
study and education. The world is our oyster; take
advantage of what is opening. It will be beneficial as we
proceed with this cycle of Saturn through the houses.

Saturn in the 4th House
It is time to sink in and build a foundation for our life's
work. Lay the groundwork for what you are here to do.
Get organized and take your time in making decisions.
Often family takes on greater significance at this time.
Responsibilities for family members may way heavier on
us. We need to take care of the home front before
branching out in the next stages.

Saturn in the 5th House
It is time to take a risk—or many risks. Leap out of the
box. Try something and fail. If we have no failures at this

time, we might not be leaping high or far enough. Take a big chance. This is a time to run with your ideas with passion. An opportunity to express yourself in public can support forward motion with your work.

Saturn in the 6th House

After the risks of Saturn in the 5th house, we now have some clarity about our path. During this stage, we get our ducks in a row. It is time to make decisions about the systems we need, and to make plans. This is the last stage when we have room to fully negotiate with the world. What we tell ourselves in the quiet of our daily decisions tells the world a lot about what we want to do with this life. Take the time to make a 10-year plan for your career/life work, being aware that a significant peak of your vocational expression occurs in ten years.

Saturn in the 7th House

The world starts talking back and pointing us in a direction. After the past 14 years when we were sending the world rockets of information about what we wanted, the world now takes all of those wants and messages and determines its best use for us. This is when we find out how our desires match with the needs of the world. Pay attention to the signs. What falls away needs to fall away. What comes into our life is likely important for the next ten years, if not longer.

Saturn in the 8th House

This is when we are tested. We may feel like the world no longer wants what we have to offer. We may want to give up. Actually, it is time to strengthen our resolve, dig deeper and listen to the messages the world is giving us about our direction. Usually, there is a paring down; something needs to be sacrificed so that we can move on. Like leaving a suitcase at the airport that was too heavy for the plane, we move through this transit more easily with simply a carry on. The need to travel lighter is *not* a sign to abandon the voyage. It is a sign that the voyage will be longer and more significant than you can imagine and right now you have too much stuff. Many times the extra stuff is a relationship that is not in our highest or doesn't match the path we are on or the path the world needs from us. The relationship may be a long one and dearly coveted, but if it isn't the right one for this journey, we will need to let it go. The suffering of this time is our resistance to seeing what truly serves us and our purpose.

Saturn in the 9th House
This is time to expand out into our vocation, to say YES! and open to the possibilities. If we have been opening and paying attention throughout the first eight stages of this cycle, then this time is confirmation and clarity on our path. If this cycle began before our Saturn return, or has included particularly difficult times, we may find ourselves unhappy with our course at this time. This is our last chance for the next five years to redirect.

Saturn in the 10th House
This is the peak phase of our career/vocational path. All of the decisions and experiences of the past 20 years have led to this moment. We have made our bed so we have to

lie in it. I find that it is very difficult to get out of our current situations during this time. It is our two to three-year period of conscription. We get to have a body this lifetime and the world wants us to come fully into what we have to offer. This is the time when the world demands that we participate in our purpose. Rarely do we find ourselves without work at this time. Responsibilities can be heavy and consuming. If we have taken big enough risks (particularly when Saturn was in the 5th house), have let go of what was holding us back (especially during the two years of Saturn was in our 8th house), we can find ourselves at a powerful epoch of success and ambition.

Saturn in the 11th House

Now that the hard work is done, we get to reap the benefits and rewards. This is a wonderful time for collaboration. This stage often brings recognition. Share freely your gifts with the world. The world will eat it up. This is a good time to consider selling a business or figuring out some way to create passive income for the next three years.

Saturn in the 12th House

It is time to release the vocation/path that we have been on for the past 26 or so years. We can bring some of this work into the next cycle, but I often find that it is best to take time off and let go of what we have been doing. The more willing we are to step into the unknown, the easier the whole next cycle will be.

Chiron Transits

Perceived Effect: Chiron offers us a chance to heal through bringing on a crisis. We are often challenged to move through an experience that brings into our awareness a feeling of hurt or pain from the past. Chiron is also an indicator of relationship changes and opening our hearts to greater love.

Lessons: Chiron is the wounded healer. With Chiron we learn to heal. In accepting our perceived challenges and wounds, we open to our capacity to heal others and ourselves. Chiron, orbiting between the visible Saturn and the invisible Uranus, is considered the bridge planet between the seen and unseen realms. It heightens our perception of what is happening in the dark. Our subconscious speaks directly to our awareness of what is real. We are able to shift unconscious patterns during a Chiron transit. In Magi astrology, Chiron is the planet of Love—the kind of love we find with a true soul mate.

Retrograde: Retrograde Chiron gives us a chance to ground and heal. Like the saying "time heals all wounds", the Chiron retrograde time offers us that kind of time. I understand that all of our memories are held somewhere in our bodies—often, if not always, in the interconnected layers of fascia that runs throughout our physical form. Like stretching after a race, the Chiron retrograde period gives us a chance to integrate the healing that has occurred through the current transit or past transits. The healing settles into our body, into the deeper layers of fascia, whether in our physical body or our energy body or both. Sometimes this is the most important time, when we allow the healing to settle in. Like after we break a bone, the bone seem like it is better because we can now put weight on it, but the deeper layers of tissue may still need time. The Chiron retrograde offers us powerful healing in perhaps a subtler or less obvious way.

Orbit: 50.36 years
Orb: 3°, larger during the retrograde period
Time it takes: About a year and a quarter.

~~~~~~~~~~~

Chiron/Sun

When Chiron transits our Sun it wakes us up to who we really are and want to be. It points out where our pride may be interfering with our fullest joy and radiance. Sometimes a health crisis at this time points out a deeper change that, once made, heals us on levels we didn't even know needed healing.

Read *You Can Heal Your Life by Louise Hay*

Chiron/Moon

The Moon holds our deepest emotional patterns. In the Moon we find our perspective, the way we process life, and what holds and secures us to this planet. When Chiron transits the Moon, our whole world may feel disrupted, because when our perspective changes, everything changes. Like ripples on a pond, the whole pond looks different even if barely anything has changed. Pay attention to what is real. Open to changing your view on the world. It is your consciousness being challenged to expand at this time.

Read *A Path with Heart: A Guide through the Perils and Promises of Spiritual Life by Jack Kornfield*

Chiron/Mercury

When Chiron transits Mercury, we have an opportunity for real alchemical healing. Where we place our focus changes. We may have been valuing one aspect of our life over other aspects. At this time, a crisis erupts that helps us change the direction of our life.

Read *The Emerald Tablet: Alchemy for Personal Transformation by Dennis William Hauck*

Chiron/Venus

This transit is particularly important to our love lives. We can meet someone significant, fall in love or fall more deeply in love with the one we are with when Chiron conjuncts, trines or quincunxes Venus. If the relationship we are in isn't true for us, isn't in our highest alignment, a crisis shows up for healing so that we can move into a truer relationship. Chiron in hard aspect, such as to Venus, more fully brings to light issues in our relationships or issues blocking us from loving fully.

Read *Embracing the Beloved: Relationship as a Path of Awakening by Stephen and Ondrea Levine*

Chiron/Mars

When Chiron transits Mars, we get to adjust how we focus our attention. This is a good time to take a look at our goals. Where are we headed? Do we want to change direction? Chiron inspires Mars to take the initiative to change direction if needed. Any crisis at this time is to help us assert our self in a direction that is more direct to where we are going, even if we don't know where that is.

Read *Emmanuel's Book: A Manual for Living Comfortably in the Cosmos by Pat Rodegast and Judith Stanton*

Chiron/Jupiter

Chiron transiting Jupiter challenges us to open to possibilities that we may have been closed to in the past. We may have strong visions at this time. The messages from the world are positive and supportive of us opening to a greater potential in our work lives and love lives. When Chiron conjuncts, trines or quincunxes Jupiter, it is another good transit for falling in love and meeting a significant other.

Read *The Seven Spiritual Laws of Success: A Practical Guide to the Fulfillment of Your Dreams* by Deepak Chopra

Chiron/Nodes

This is a profound time of healing our souls. Souls are the vibrational imprint—the patterns of lives before and to come—that is the foundation for this life. Every soul has memory and this memory feeds and repeats the patterns of the past. There is always healing on this life journey that takes us into greater freedom where we are no longer bound to these vibrational imprints. When Chiron joins the **South Node**, the past life memory arises to be healed. It will most likely arise in the form of a challenge to a familiar way of being, something we have taken for granted and accepted as fact or real. But this thing is asking to be changed. We are clearing something old so that we can open to a new life. Chiron on the **North Node** offers us vision, an ability to move on. The crisis that is arising is pointing out where we have limited ourselves or set our sites on a dream that is too small. Time to open up. When Chiron squares the Nodes, the challenge may be more intense and confrontational. We have to move from the past life patterns of the South Node into the highest manifestation of the North Node potential that we can.

Read *The Holographic Universe* by Michael Talbot

Chiron/Saturn

Chiron challenges our view of reality when it transits Saturn. We have to be willing to adjust to the truth that is presented in a particularly confrontational way, especially if it is one of the hard aspects. This transit is particularly difficult on relationships. We are asked to heal an old pattern—so old that we don't even recognize it as a pattern. We think what needs to change is something core to who we are. But the only thing really core to who we are is love. Most everything else is something we have developed to compensate for something else. Be willing to heal. Whatever is called into question at this time is likely something we would be better off changing anyway.

Read *Refuge by Terry Tempest Williams*

Chiron/Chiron

During these transits, how we heal is called into focus. The old wound, the one we came into this life to heal, is opened up for deeper healing. Sometimes health issues related to old injuries, both physical and emotional, are triggered at this time. Look for the new path of healing that may help us move into even greater awareness of who we are.

Read *Hands of Light: A Guide to Healing Through the Human Energy Field by Barbara Brennan, Illustrated by Jos. A. Smith*

Chiron/Uranus

These outer/outer transits happen at levels that can be hard to see or understand. This is a powerful transit for spiritual awakenings. Both Chiron and Uranus are related to the Kundalini energy that rises and falls along the spine, that opens us to greater consciousness.

Read *Awakening Shakti: The Transformative Power of the Goddesses of Yoga by Sally Kempton*

Chiron/Neptune

This can be a confusing time since the healing that is happening is related to deep subconscious dreams and issues. We may feel more sensitive to what is happening in the world. We are opening to love more fully. When Chiron conjuncts, trines or quincunxes Neptune, we are more open to love and relationship. Deep soul connections can form during that time.

Read *Path of Empowerment: Pleiadian Wisdom for a World in Chaos by Barbara Marciniak*

Chiron/Pluto

This is time for healing some deep-seated issues. Chiron brings out Pluto's bad side, opening up fears and old losses. If there is loss from the past that we haven't quite dealt with, this transit will help bring it up and out. This is a good year for therapy. Something that has been blocking us for a long time can be transformed. Chiron as the healer can dredge up the demons and this is the time when Chiron has the most access to them. Remember that this is one of those times that can seem scarier than it is. The dark side is the disowned part of us begging to be witnessed. Be willing to see and accept what arises at this time.

Read *Healing Pluto Problems by Donna Cunningham*

117

Chiron/Ascendant

The Ascendant rules the physical body, so this is one of the transits that may bring on a health crisis. This health issue is here to tap into longer-term issues so that they can be healed. This is a good time to make changes in our outer appearance so that what we are presenting to the world aligns with the internal experience of love and happiness that we long to have. When Chiron joins the Descendant, it is time to take a closer look at our relationships. A long-held pattern of denial may get a rude awakening. Chiron brings things into the light to be explored, examined and healed. Let the healing in your relationships begin. Chiron transits typically last a year, so think of it as a year to heal.

Use *Love is in the Earth: A Kaleidoscope of Crystals by Melody* to look into using crystals for healing.

Chiron/Midheaven

Time to take a closer look at our vocation, our calling in life. When Chiron joins the Midheaven, we may get called to be a healer if that is in our natal chart. This can be the time we have been waiting for in order to hang out our shingle as a healer. Chiron can support us in getting freed from a limiting idea of what is possible for us with our work or career. When Chiron joins the IC, it may be time to make a move. Our home life may come into a certain level of disarray as the pieces of our life get rearranged. Ask yourself if you are in the right location for what you really want in your life.

Read *The Road Less Traveled: A New Psychology of Love, Traditional Values and Spiritual Growth by M. Scott Peck, M.D.*

~~~~~~~~~~

Stones for a challenging Chiron transit:
When we are having a difficult time with Chiron it is often the fear of suffering, either physically or emotionally, that is driving the challenge. **Amber** is a good stone for transforming fear into excitement. **Aquamarine** calms our nervous systems. **Tourmaline**, a good stone for deep healing, can support intense fears moving into catharsis and transformation. **Lapis Lazuli** supports us in manifesting our truest experience, helping a Chiron transit stay in motion toward the healing we crave. **Celestite** assists us in seeing a bigger picture so that the crisis we are in has meaning and relevance. **Amazonite** brings the Chiron transit into a new level of experience, where the healing becomes mystical.

Chiron through the Houses

Chiron takes 51 years to make its journey around the Sun and Earth. It spends about 4 ¼ years in each sign and about that in each house. Chiron points out what we need to heal. Every four plus years we get to review a different area of our life and dive into the issues that that area presents.

Chiron in the 1st House
We process issues around identity and our sense of self. We find ourselves asking the question "who am I?" and receiving a new answer.

Chiron in the 2nd House

Financial challenges at this time help us get clear about what we really want in life. Where we focus our intention is where the energy, aka money, follows. Notice where your attention is focused. If money challenges show up now, they are to heal past life issues of scarcity and fears about survival.

Chiron in the 3rd House

We are healing early childhood wounds, especially concerning our early childhood education. Those first precious years of school can set us on a path of success or indulge us with challenges that take years to shake. This is a time to shake them off and move on. Challenge yourself to learn something new.

Chiron in the 4th House

Family drama that arises at this time serves us to heal early wounds around attachment, either lack of attachment or over-attachment. Our parents may need or want more support at this time. Issues are often passed down from generation to generation, and healing can be passed upward and backward through the generations. We may be called to heal at this time a generational wound, an issue that was handed down to us from our ancestors.

Chiron in the 5th House

Chiron traveling through our 5th house highlights blocks to our creative expression and issues with our children if we have them. Many of us feel challenged to share our art and creativity with the world. We fear public speaking and put ourselves down for not being artistic or special. Now is the time to get over that and let your light shine. Take a risk to share your particular gift with the world.

Chiron in the 6th House

A physical healing crisis at this time can reveal old issues. A back injury in childhood may be triggered by a simple fall or the wrong twist of the neck. The beauty of this transit is that the activation of old health issues can be healed. Deeper wounds come to the surface and we are able to reach and transform the source of the wound. This is an excellent time to focus on healing your body.

Chiron in the 7th House

Chiron loves "true love" and during this time, Chiron wants us to find it. Whether we find it in the current relationship we are in or whether we have to go looking elsewhere, Chiron doesn't let us settle for less than truth. Couples therapy at this time can work wonders.

Chiron in the 8th House

Chiron in the 8th begs us to take a deep look at any abuses we may have experienced in childhood. Sexual trauma at this time may reveal sex abuse in childhood. While this may be a deep dive into looking at our history of trauma, Chiron serves us to open to truly loving ourselves and healing shame. This is a time when we may need to come out of the closet. Healing can take many forms, and being willing to reveal our true selves can support Chiron in working its healing magic.

Chiron in the 9th House
The awakening time helps us get out into the world to have more experiences and learn new things. This is a good time to take a trip with a purpose of uncovering some unique part of yourselves. Do your own eat, pray, love journey.

Chiron in the 10th House
Wake up and find your true calling. Chiron highlights the aspects of our work that are dragging us down. Pay attention to your resistance. Whatever you resist is giving you information into what you are healing. Something is getting in your way of success. Chiron is here to help you release any blockages to vocational fulfillment.

Chiron in the 11th House
Drama can unfold during any Chiron transit and during this time, drama in our circle of friends and community is the focus. We can find out who are true friends are during this time. Don't be hasty in throwing out a good friendship. The issue that arises at this time is so that we can heal something in ourselves that is getting in the way of healthy relationship. Do the work to heal the friendship.

Chiron in the 12th House
This is time for focus on our spiritual lives. Take some time to retreat and dive deeper into your spiritual path. Develop a daily spiritual practice that honors your path and helps you move into a more peaceful state of mind.

Uranus Transits

Perceived Effect: Uranus appears to change everything in its path. It seems to excite, enliven and stir up anything that is trying to sleep or hide. It is the energy of Shakti running up and down our spines. It is a time when the world seems out of our hands and when things appear to be spinning out of control. Lean into the electrical, excitement of the Uranus transit and fear can be transformed into joy.

Lessons: Uranus teaches us that the Universe is a big place and that lots is going on and that even when we think we have control we do not. Uranus teaches us to let go and experience the joy and fullness of life. Uranus teaches us that trying to hold on ultimately never works. Uranus teaches us that security is really the ability we have to trust in life and ourselves—because everything, even ourselves, is changing. Ultimately Uranus teaches us, that much like a fractal, what may appear as chaotic and random is in truth the Universe working in perfect harmony.

Retrograde: When Uranus moves retrograde, the shifting, changing nature of Uranus goes inward. The changes are felt more internally, in our intimate lives and in the underground of the planet.

Stationing: Stationing Uranus is one to watch. Uranus when it stations can wreak all kinds of havoc. Our nervous systems can easily get overwhelmed. Our wires get an extra jolt of electricity. If we can stay calm and grounded, the energy will pass through blissfully. (Remember, it is just energy.)

Orbit: Uranus takes 83.75 Earth-years to get around the Sun. It almost rotates totally on its side and its day lasts 17.2 Earth hours.
Orb: 2°, larger during the retrograde period once it has already begun the transit
Time it takes: About a year and a half.

~~~~~~~~~~

Uranus/Sun

Uranus wants us to feel more alive—so whatever it takes to get us to want to live, Uranus is here for us in that way. Whatever we are holding onto which is diminishing our thirst for life, our overall well-being or our spiritual growth, Uranus helps that to change and shift. Say "Hurray!" to whatever goes during an Uranus/Sun transit.

Read *The Four Fold Way: Walking the Paths of the Warrior, Teacher, Healer and Visionary by Angeles Arrien*

Uranus/Moon

Uranus serves to trigger events that stir us emotionally. Wherever we may be emotionally blocked—where the energy of our emotions is not allowing us to process great joy and love—that is where Uranus will strike. Get out the tissues and the party banners.

Read *A Thousand Names for Joy: Living in Harmony with the Way Things Are by Byron Katie and Stephen Mitchell*

Uranus/Mercury

Uranus opens our minds to understand and think through all kinds of new and interesting stuff. This can be an incredible transit for writing, learning, inventing, and speaking or just sharing new concepts and ideas with others.

Read *The Seat of the Soul by Gary Zukav*

Uranus/Venus

In case your love life is boring, Uranus waves through to put a little kick in it. We may have a wild romance or an unexpected change in a current relationship. In case we were overly attached to a person or possession, Uranus can come in to help us let go. This can be a wonderfully creative time. Enjoy your eccentricity. Love change.

Read *The Mayan Code: Time Acceleration and Awakening the World Mind* by Barbara Hand Clow

Uranus/Mars
Our actions may have unintended consequences at this time. Uranus teaches us that, indeed, we do attract the perfect situations to us in order that we may feel more alive and in touch with a greater presence than our ordinary 3-D reality. Accidents of many kinds may be experienced during these transits, especially if we are ungrounded. Stay in touch with your body. You are learning how you create your reality and the situations that come to you. Stay tuned into your re-actions during this transit, especially the feeling of frustration and anger that may arise suddenly and for no apparent reason. Watch and learn—many important lessons can come through this transit. Eat well and stay as embodied as possible. Slow down if the world feels like it is spinning.

Read *The Way of the Peaceful Warrior: A Book That Changes Lives* by Dan Millman

Uranus/Jupiter
Uranus activates the part of us that wants more out of life. We want to expand, grow, travel, and experience new things. Go and enjoy without overdoing as things can get a little out of control with these two hooking up.

Read *Light from Guru to Disciple* by Rajarshi Muni

Uranus/Nodes

This is Soul Wake Up time. We may experience a sense of things falling apart initially, something unraveling or changing from a simple, sudden, unexpected event. This is a year when we are stepping into greater aliveness through what appears as chaos but really is simply a restructuring so that we can move into greater freedom and creativity in our lives.

Read *Siddhartha by Hermann Hesse*

Uranus/Saturn

Uranus wants us to deal with some lurking authority issues. Any place where we have projected authority onto someone else gets a good kick in the pants. Uranus challenges us to accept responsibility for our lives, our paths and our past. Then, it helps us move on. Any Saturn blocks or old karma may resurrect to be transformed for good. Enjoy the rush of release when you get to say good-bye to some old barrier to happiness.

Read *The Stranger by Albert Camus*

Uranus/Chiron

An old wound is arises to be healed at a deeper level. Uranus sends shock waves through a callous, melts the gluing in congealed muscle and sends heat and light into any rheumatic experiences we are having. This is a wonderful time to seek out alternative therapies for healing. Under the guidance of Uranus they can work especially well.

Read *Conscious Caregiving by Carol Trasatto*

Uranus/Uranus

Awakening itself, Uranus helps us to accept change. Our energy body is awakened. Shakti runs through us. If we are stuck, we get to feel how it might feel to unstick ourselves. Our soul journey and our purpose on Earth are heightened. Changes occur so that we might re-align and accept that what feels out of control is just our own insecurity. Move on. Uranus has no time for in-security or the desire for circumstances to make us feel secure. Especially enjoy the Uranus opposition at 40 to 42 years of age, when our energy body goes through an important change. That is when we can accept more energy without the need to stuff it some place else. This transit is the transit most often associated with the typical mid-life crisis, when we want to buy a sports car or leave our wives for a younger woman. The energy is surging through us and if we lack imagination we go for the typical youthful things that our culture has to offer. Resist the urge to play out old fantasies and awaken instead to the purpose of your life.

Read *Everything Is Here to Help You: A Loving Guide to Your Soul's Evolution by Matt Kahn*

Uranus/Neptune

An outer planet transiting an outer planet is often a generational shift and one that may be subtler in actual personal experience. Neptune in our natal chart shows us what we are releasing and letting go of in this lifetime. Uranus can awaken shifts and help us with letting go. There is also the chance that psychic abilities and our intuition may be heightened at this time. Spiritual opening and "Aha's!" are likely and welcome.

Read *The Purposeful Universe: How Quantum Theory and Mayan Cosmology Explain the Origin and Evolution of Life by Carl Johan Calleman, Ph. D.*

Uranus/Pluto

Like the 1960's when these two were conjunct, Uranus wants deep revolutionary change that moves all of us into the next stage of evolution. Life must evolve and Pluto represents that deep transformation. Uranus helps us wake up and get there.

Read *The Rights of Man by Thomas Paine*

Uranus/Ascendant

Uranus crosses the Ascendant every 84 years, so it is a once-in-a-lifetime event. Uranus asks us to make a big life change. We are starting a new journey. Our personality may change unexpectedly. We can change everything during this transit. A sudden, unexpected event shifts our perspective on life and we may choose to change our circumstances dramatically.

Read *Das Energi by Paul Williams*

Uranus/Midheaven

When Uranus conjuncts the MC, big career changes might be in store for you. At the very least, be prepared for some kind of unexpected shake up. Uranus always wants us to come into right alignment. When Uranus crosses the MC, the unexpected changes serve the purpose of getting us unstuck from a work situation that is either not serving us or not serving the world. When Uranus crosses the IC, it is often time for a move or at least a really good house cleaning. Sometimes the unexpected is unpleasant in the short term but the long term is supportive of us moving into a better situation for our soul work. Uranus squaring the MC and IC can set off more challenging changes that bring us into a better alignment with both work and home. Any imbalance between home and work life often becomes more stressful and then breaks open for us to make the necessary shift.

Read *The Hitchhiker's Guide to the Galaxy by Douglas Adams*

~~~~~~~~~~~

Stones for a challenging Uranus transit:
Uranus transits usually want us to be able to experience more energy—they light us up through offering an experience of change and 'out-of-controlness". This is to help us move through life with greater ease—the more energy we can handle, the more joy and happiness we can experience. **Amber** helps align the electrical fields in our bodies, helps us to use the energy pulsing through us and be available for more energy. **Aquamarine** is a calming stone and supports the nervous system in remaining calm. It is not a very powerful stone but can help if the energy is too much and we just need to chill. **Celestite** is also known for relieving anxiety and supporting calm while it also enhances creativity and a sense of possibility.

Uranus through the Houses

The cycle of Uranus around the Sun and through the twelve houses takes 84 years, which divides nicely by twelve to make seven-year stages. Currently, 84 years is about the human life expectancy. The Uranus cycle most closely correlates with twelve stages of our life. As Uranus moves through the houses, it starts with the house that Uranus is in in your natal chart. That house becomes your own personal beginning and end.

Uranus in the 1st House

Time for a radical change in our identity. All things can change during this time. Step out of the box of convention and dare to be different.

Uranus in the 2nd House

Finances can go up and down. Sudden windfalls and sudden downfalls can accompany this time. If we are clinging to security, this can be painful. If we are opening to a more radical and alive life, then the changes support us in feeling more radiant and joyful.

Uranus in the 3rd House

This is a great time for studying new subjects. Our minds are opened and we can have great ideas at this time.

Uranus in the 4th House

Our home life may be a bit more chaotic and less stable at this time. Time to make a big move.

Uranus in the 5th House
Open up the creative expressive channels. Take a chance to be fully expressed in this world.

Uranus in the 6th House
We may feel more challenged with our health and job during this time. The 6th house likes stability and routine and Uranus does everything to upset those things. We may feel more anxious. This is a good time to change unhealthy habits.

Uranus in the 7th House
For seven years, we are opening to a relationship that is more alive, exciting and true to who we are. Accept the changes and watch what appears in the vacancies that Uranus creates.

Uranus in the 8th House
Unexpected changes in our work and financial lives serve to empower us in the world.

Uranus in the 9th House
Time to journey to foreign lands for no reason. Time to learn and teach and open to the wildness of this one precious life.

Uranus in the 10th House
Our work lives may feel unstable at this time unless we are working in an area that is inherently creative, unique, out-of-the-box and revolutionary. Allow yourself to trigger the revolution and open to greater freedom.

Uranus in the 11th House

Uranus loves the 11th house and feels free to create radical change in our connections with others. This is a time of enhanced freedom. You may notice that friendships that no longer support your highest, suddenly take a turn in a different direction.

Uranus in the 12th House

We are coming to a close with this Uranus cycle. We may feel lost and confused. Unless we are on a spiritual path and have our bearings in the unseen realms, we may find the upsets and changes of this time confusing. We are learning to use our intuition more effectively.

THE WHIRLING DANCE OF PLANETS

Neptune Transits

Perceived Effect: In transit, Neptune shows us what we need to let go of, what we are overly attached to that is no longer serving us, and offers us the experience of feeling disoriented so that we can find our true path. Like playing pin-the-tail-on-the-donkey, we are blindfolded and turned around several times and then given a task. The disorientation helps us to dislodge stuck ways of thinking, behavior patterns that have become engrained and emotional tendencies that keep us from experiencing all the love that is available.

135

Lessons: Ultimately, Neptune wants us to experience love—big love—true love—divine love. Neptune wants us to be awakened and know that we are all interconnected. Neptune serves by opening us to compassion for others, and ourselves by opening our intuitive faculties and giving us a chance to exercise our psychic muscles.

Retrograde: Not much noticeable difference compared with direct motion. We may feel that our creative urges are more internally felt and that we are swimming backwards in the stream of life.

Stationing: The effect of Neptune stationing may be likened to the experience of being underwater, in a storm or lost at sea. Neptune is asking us to trust our intuition completely blindfolded.

Orbit: 164.8 years
Orb: 2° (more during retrograde periods)
Time it takes: Two years.

~~~~~~~~~~

Neptune/Sun

Any concepts we carry about our self-needs can be released when Neptune transits the Sun. Attachments, control issues and any need for external security is deeply challenged. We may need to wait and ride the waves of this transit before anything that looks like progress can be accomplished. This is a time to put things on hold and allow ourselves full access to the unknown. We may feel more tired. We may feel less energized and vital. At the same time, if we open to the flow and exercise our intuition we may find ourselves on a big wave that takes us far and wide into un-charted and exciting territory. This is a time of spiritual awakenings and increased access to Love, God and the Great Unknown.

Read *The Upanishads Introduced & Translated by Eknath Easwaran*

Neptune/Moon

This is a transit that in some way is altering our psychic abilities. Whether we are in touch with it or not we all have psychic abilities. The Moon in our chart is how we experience the world, our senses, our ability to process reality and how we receive information. Neptune asks us at this time to open to receiving information from a higher plane—take it from the Universe, from divine inspiration and let go of the baggage that has limited our perception of what is possible. We may be asked to clear out early childhood issues, let go of old patterns from abusive relationships and release any patterns originating in childhood experiences.

Read *The Untethered Soul: The Journey Beyond Yourself by Michael A. Singer*

Neptune/Mercury

When Neptune transits our Mercury, we may feel like our mind has gone on a vacation. The words may be hard to find—our tongue lost in the back of our mouth. Our creative life may be enhanced. It is time to open to irrational thinking and follow our gut impulses and learn from them. We may need to give ourselves a break from logic during this transit. It can also be helpful if we let go of expectations of how we communicate and express ourselves. Like most Neptune transits, a good long retreat is the best medicine.

Read *Illusions: The Adventures of a Reluctant Messiah by Richard Bach*

Neptune/Venus

This is a very creative time and a transit with great potential for falling into love, falling into the creative experience and having a deep desire for beauty. The planet of divine love triggers the planet of human love and we are asked to merge our human experience with our spiritual path. We may feel we are in a fog and our relationships may seem unreal. Illusions are likely and we may not be able to see reality through the mists. If we can fully participate in our artistic abilities, this can be a transit of wonder. Wait 'til the fog clears before making any Saturn-like commitments. In other words, fall deeply in love, but don't join your bank accounts until after the transit is over. Neptune conjunct, trine or quincunx Venus are the most auspicious transits for meeting a significant other. Neptune oppose or square Venus may bring in relationships that are initially disappointing but ultimately transcendent with a great chance for healing deep wounds.

Read *Goddesses: Mysteries of the Feminine Divine by Joseph Campbell*

THE WHIRLING DANCE OF PLANETS

Neptune/Mars

The initiatory energy of Mars must move through deep water before getting anything done. Neptune teaches our Mars to be patient. We must weather the storms and wait on the Tao. This is a transit of transcendence. We must move through the ethereal realms in order to make something happen. Our own urge to go forth and make something happen may get lost in a sea of confusion. We try something and find we have fallen into the pool. Let it go. Move into the middle of the stream and flow with the power of the river.

Read *Don't Push the River: It Flows by Itself* by Barry Stevens

Neptune/Jupiter

When these two get together our visions of life, as we know it get a little out of hand. We want to expand straight out of the cosmos. We understand large concepts of life. This is a time to wander—to wander in the land of philosophy, wander through foreign countries and wander through out-of-print books. As we let go of thinking small, we may find ourselves with a completely different perspective on the world. We may need to get our hands dirty in the earth for grounding—or spend some serious time in nature.

Read *Leaves of Grass* by Walt Whitman

Neptune/Nodes

When Neptune transits the Nodes, we have a profound opportunity to change past-life patterns. To access Neptune's healing properties, a daily, routine spiritual practice is often necessary. Without the discipline of Saturn, Neptune gets lost and when Neptune steps on the Nodes, this lost experience can take us for a wild ride. The Moon's nodes in the natal chart indicate the places where we are most likely to take a detour in life by getting distracted with desire. In our world, we have so much opportunity to be distracted by our desires. Advertising is the art of coopting our desire nature and manipulating it so that we follow their lead. The work of this transit is to claim responsibility for our desire and use it as a lead to know where our truest soul work lies. In order to claim this responsibility, it is important to recognize when our desire is being coopted. Taking time away from media, an almost impossible feat in this current world, may be the most helpful thing we do for our psyches during this transit of psychic work.

Read *Light on the Yoga Sutras of Patanjali by B.K.S. Iyengar*

Neptune/Saturn

Neptune is asking Saturn, the authority in our chart, to take a deeper look at how it is running things. We are asked to be more fluid and less rigid during this time. We are focused on being loving rather than stern. We are challenged to accept that no matter how hard we try, external security will never satisfy the need for inner security. The more energy we put into creating external security during this transit, the more likely we are to experience the very thing that could take it all away. This is a time to trust our own ability to write our lives just the way we are called to.

Read *How the World Is Made: The Story of Creation according to Sacred Geometry by John Michell and Allan Brown*

Neptune/Chiron

This is a transit that may lie beneath the surface like a sleeping dragon. We may not even see or know its effects until we have unwittingly stumbled into the dragon's lair and awakened a deep and old wound that longs to be healed through the mystical power of prayer, meditation and love. Don't try to figure it out. Only diving deep into the unknown territory of the spirit-body connection will allow healing during this transit.

Read *Cell Level Meditation: Breathing with The Wisdom & Intelligence of The Cell by Patricia Kay, MA and Barry Grundland, MD*

Neptune/Uranus

Since any Neptune transit is supporting us in having a deeper experience of the oneness of the Universe, this transit is showing us how that oneness is part of the change and chaos that we create as we disrupt old patterns. Uranus in our natal chart tells us how, when and where to set off the changes that are needed in our lives to release prior life patterning. When Neptune transits this place, we are shown through visions and experiences how we need to change so that the stagnant cellular memories can be awakened into flowing and joyous health.

Read *The Spiritual Teachings of Ramana Maharshi by Ramana Maharshi*

Neptune/Neptune

This is a time of deep questioning. We are called to re-evaluate our life. We need to ask, "What is our great vision for this life?" The feelings of longing and desire may be more awakened than usual and we may find ourselves wandering around in a stupor. This transit is an inner journey. The terrains of the soul are often strange and illogical. We are asked to follow our intuition, to pay attention to the memories and dreams that seem to arise out of nowhere. These dreams are indications of the places in our life where we are neglecting our spirit. Reading the signs is not a matter of research, but of allowing our intuition full reign.

Read *The Universal One by Walter Russell*. You may not have heard of this lesser known philosopher and scientist, but this was a life-changing book for me.

Neptune/Pluto

Neptune, during this transit, wants us to experience our power and truth with kindness and compassion. This is a deep underwater transit that may remain deep within the unseen realms of our psyche unless we have access to these realms through creative endeavors, healing modalities and spiritual and/or divination practices—to mention a few ways. This is a transit that may feel in general strange until we are still—completely still inside. Then we can see the jewels.

Read *A Gradual Awakening by Stephen Levine*

Neptune/Ascendant

When Neptune conjuncts the Ascendant, this is a hugely

significant time in our life. Since this transit only happens once in a lifetime, and for less than half of the population, it is a transit that is perfectly designed just for your particular karma. It is a transit that is meant to break us open through having to be present with the vast unknown. We can easily feel overwhelmed with the uncertainty of our life. Neptune's intention is to bring us more into the experience of Love. Any place in our being where we are denying ourselves love will be highlighted and torn down. We might not be able to see clearly at this time and we might feel unseen. However, something quite magical and mystical is working through our field of intention. Let it. With Neptune, we always have to just allow the transit to happen. There is often nothing we can do about whatever circumstances we find ourselves in. When Neptune crosses the Descendant, we are asked to look at the mystery of partnership, of our work in relationship and release any illusions that someone else can make us feel whole. Ultimately, the work is to clear the illusion of fear and open more deeply into trust—trust in the big Divine plan that is only partially visible.

Read *The Power of Now by Eckhart Tolle*

Neptune/Midheaven

When Neptune crosses the MC, we might experience our career dissolving, goals we have worked hard for may seem farther out of reach. Yet, this is just the beginning. Neptune is offering us a new vision, a new path, one that will serve the greater good and our own unique soul work more abundantly. Neptune can come in like a storm, but it leaves us with a new perspective on life. When Neptune crosses the IC, we may have an uneasy feeling that where we are living needs to change. It may take us the full two-year transit to know our true calling in our home and family life. As always with Neptune, allow the mystery, follow your intuition and let the old stuck places go. Neptune squares the MC and IC asks us to work out the balance between home and work. We ultimately must come into a better alignment with both.

Read *The Soul's Code: In Search of Character and Calling* by *James Hillman*

~~~~~~~~~~~

Stones for a challenging Neptune transit:
When Neptune is challenging we often feel disoriented, confused and tired. If you are feeling extra spacey, use a grounding and focusing stone like **Calcite** or **Citrine**. If you are opening and having extraordinary spiritual experiences, use **Apophyllite** for visions and **Celestite** for harnessing the creative potential of the transit. **Spectrolite** can be helpful for channeling the etheric-plane energy that runs in abundance during Neptune transits. Spectrolite will assist with being able to clearly and consciously direct this energy. **Jet** and **Hematite** are also helpful during Neptune transits since we often need extra protection when we are spacey and ungrounded.

Neptune through the Houses

As Neptune moves through the houses, it shares with us the interconnectedness of all life and challenges us to trust that the Universe will catch us.

Neptune in the 1st House
Our identity changes to become one with our spiritual truth. It is time to be more generous and altruistic. Our ego may get a lashing. Take it in stride. Ultimately, we can't take it with us.

Neptune in the 2nd House
For us westerners, this can be a challenging time because the longing for security meets the need to trust that we can't always get what we want, but we always get what we need.

Neptune in the 3rd House
Take time to immerse in esoteric studies. The mysteries of the world have deeper meaning for us at this time.

Neptune in the 4th House
We are learning that home is where the heart is. Relax into trusting that we are held on the planet no matter where we live.

Neptune in the 5th House
Allow yourself to express yourself. This can be a very creative and mystical time.

Neptune in the 6th House
We may find less attachment to worldly life at this time. Meanwhile our bodies still need nourishment and support, possibly even more now that usual. Take greater care of your body at this time.

Neptune in the 7th House
In this world, with its constant dream of romance, Neptune in the 7th makes us extra dreamy and gullible in relationship. Allow yourself to fall in love and then allow yourself to see the truth.

Neptune in the 8th House
Neptune entreats us to discover the deeper mysteries in life. Our dream life can offer solutions and understandings that support our spiritual unfolding.

Neptune in the 9th House
A wonderful time for pilgrimages and spiritual journeys of all kinds. We may feel like we are wandering. Allow yourself to find a new path.

Neptune in the 10th House
Our vocational lives may be murky at this time. We may have a hard time finding what the calling is. Like all Neptune transits, the answer lies in patience, trust and releasing control.

Neptune in the 11th House
This is a time of sharing and participating in universal love. We can find our tribe and life mates during this time.

Neptune in the 12th House

Neptune is a planet that loves the 12th house and does its best magic when it is here. Feel the calling of a spiritual life and give in to it.

Pluto Transits

Perceived Effect: Pluto asks for nothing less than complete transformation. We must clear the slate, destroy the old and create a new way of life. Any obstruction to knowing our true nature will be tested, destroyed and leveled. Pluto takes no prisoners and lets no one go. It is relentlessly demanding. Yet, it is also the most giving of the planets since this God of the Underworld also supports us in receiving joy, ecstasy and love.

Lessons: Pluto teaches us to surrender and let go. I tell people during a Pluto transit that to appease this god, intentionally let go of stuff. Go through your closet. Get rid of old things that may contain a presence that is sustaining a pattern that is getting in the way of truth, power and love. Get rid of obstructions. And, willingly and lovingly, surrender to the unknown and the magic tide of transmutation that Pluto often brings into our lives.

Pluto comes out of the Underworld to visit Earth and Humanity. If Pluto, the God of Death, comes knocking on your door, take a deep breath, invite her in, look her in the eyes and give her your fears and pain. That is what she is looking for. Pluto nudges, then demands, then destroys, in order to take away our fears. It is funny how she is the least wanted guest and yet has the most to offer.

Retrograde: While the retrograde period of Pluto may not feel much different from its direct phase, the retrograde time is a time of ascension. Pluto is ascending and offering hope and richness when it moves backwards. Pluto *retrograde* is about the resurrection from the underworld, the revelation of what was hidden, the realization of another perspective, and seeing the truth. (Pluto *direct* is about the descent into the underworld, land of hidden treasures.)

Stationing: Pluto stationing tends to stir up the water from the bottom of the well. We need to look at the underlying issues. What is behind the curtain? What are we afraid to reveal to ourselves or to another? Often times I notice people feeling like they are going through deep emotional crises during Pluto stationing. Pluto rules the endocrine system and is connected to our hormonal cycles. So take this time to nurture your hormonal state and stay tuned to whatever you are aware of that affects your hormonal cycle.

Orbit: 248 years
Orb: 2°, more during retrograde periods
Time it takes: Two to three years.

~~~~~~~~~~~

Pluto/Sun

This is one of the most important transits a person undergoes in a life. Pluto transits our Sun in the 8th harmonic once every 20 to 30 years. In our lifetime it will only conjunct or oppose our Sun once (unless we live well over 100). The Pluto transit of the Sun is a time of directly and intensely looking at who we are in this crazy mixed-up world. Everything is deep. We must come to accept and understand our true essence. We are asked at this time to let go and let what is no longer necessary for our true soul's journey to go. Something must die. If we can let it go, the journey can be beautiful, magical and remarkable. Yet often, what we are asked to let go of is something we hold dear and something we believe to be part of us. The journey of Pluto crossing the Sun is one of "I am not this"—we learn many things that we thought we were but which we are not through the loss or transformation of those identifiable things.

Read *Cosmic Consciousness: A Study in the Evolution of the Human Mind* by Richard Maurice Bucke, M.D.

Pluto/Moon

This is a very significant transit for discovering what is essential for sustaining our life force. We may find that what we thought we needed, we no longer need. We may discover an inner resource of strength that we did not know we had. Typically these lessons are accompanied by some experience or experiences that point out to us attachments that no longer serve our true selves. In fact, this is a journey *to* our true selves—the true self we did not even know existed. Know that whatever is being cleared in our lives is getting in the way of a deeper experience of joy and passion in life.

Read *When Things Fall Apart: Heart Advice for Difficult Times* by Pema Chodron

Pluto/Mercury

Get ready to think differently about everything. You may feel like you are going mad—recognize that your cognitive abilities are going through a deep transformation. The way you process and decode information is radically changing. If you have had an excellent memory, you may find yourself forgetting things. If you have often forgotten things, you may find yourself with an excellent memory. You may have to adjust your schedule, your plans and the way you organize your life. You may have to accept that you are not what you think. Indeed, we are asked to open to information at a higher level during this transit—to accept that there is a bigger picture that we may not be able to see.

Read *The Wizard of Us: Transformational Lessons From Oz* by Jean Houston

Pluto/Venus

Learning to love, to open to love and to be in the bliss of a fully creative and/or sexual state, is what we so often desire and yet often find elusive. This transit is all set up for us to find our bliss through the utter destruction of whatever is getting in our way. Our desire is always sending messages to the Universe about what we want. Our desire comes out of our karma, our actions and experiences. Our ability to magnetize what we want is supported by our ability to be aware of and resonate with our desire. If we remain unconscious of our desire or we deny this longing, we unconsciously deny ourselves the manifestation of it. This time period is about aligning that which we long for with that which we are.

Read *Wishes Fulfilled: Mastering the Art of Manifesting* by *Wayne Dyer*

Pluto/Mars

This is a time when we are asked to look at how we align our will with the greater will of the cosmos. There is a flow in life—a grand plan so to speak. When Pluto transits Mars, we must direct our efforts toward a much greater experience of ourselves than what we had previously thought. We need to let go of controlling how this experience will come through. Our power exists within our ability to see that we are part of a much bigger plan than we imagined. When we see that we have a part to play in this great world and that only we can play that part, we find this transit to be enlivening and rich. If we resist by trying to keep ourselves small, we may find a level of frustration and rage that we did not know we were capable of experiencing. Let the rage move through your body. Experience the power that is unleashed in the experience of fire.

Read *The Hero's Journey by Joseph Campbell*

Pluto/Jupiter

Our ideals and beliefs may go through a radical dissolution process. We may find that what we "knew" to be before is not as "real" as we thought. We may leave or enter a new religion and religious beliefs may take on more or less significance. Ultimately, what we have believed to be true in our lives is completely changing. Be prepared for grief, as these beliefs may likely have been very dear to us. While these beliefs served a purpose, it is likely that they are no longer needed. We may go through a period of sustained suspension while we seek to find a new way to create our reality.

Read *The Tibetan Book of Living and Dying by Sogyal Rinpoche*

Pluto/Nodes

When Pluto transits the Nodes we are asked to do significant soul searching. What is our true purpose this lifetime? We are asked to clear the past and open to that which is most difficult for us, the thing that we resist or avoid because it doesn't come easily. The Soul Direction is something that we have not fully explored. It is the work we have come into this life to do and it isn't meant to come naturally. The work of the past lives is what comes easily and we can use that to bring our gifts into the world in service to others. The soul direction keeps haunting us until we say Yes to it. Pluto demands the Yes during this transit. When Pluto crosses the South Node we are ending cycles of the karma related to the South Node. When Pluto crosses the North Node, we are asked to fully step into our soul work without hesitation or resistance. It is the resistance in this transit that is most difficult. Pluto helps us clear out of the way whatever is holding us back. In this time, what we must let go of may seem strange. The Soul isn't always obvious or sensical in what it needs. Allow the "dark night of the soul" to be a time of greater awakening to the truth of your absolute lovability.

Read *Conscious Evolution by Barbara Marx Hubbard*

Pluto/Saturn

During this time the very foundations and concepts upon which we have built our reality are shifting. Some aspects of our life, which we have taken for granted may require transformation. There are premises that we have accepted all of our lives that now come into question as some event or new understanding of life sends a quake through our existence. As with all Pluto transits, if we are being asked to let something go, it is best to let it go as soon as possible. Pluto doesn't stop until it gets what it wants. During such a time, when something must die, let it die.

Read *Falling into Grace: Insights on the End of Suffering by Adyashanti*

Pluto/Chiron

Pluto dancing with our Chiron can be like getting bit by a snake. In order to heal we need to suck the poison out, and this may hurt more than the wound itself. Pluto helps us suck the poison out of our wounds and there is no way around it. Suck the poison out or die. Like all Pluto transits, it's about letting go, clearing and allowing something radically new to grow in its place. Don't be afraid to see the places where you have cellular memory of pain. This is a prime time for getting to the root of an issue, bringing it to the surface where it can heal and moving into a new life free from the old stuck places.

Read *World as Love, World as Self: A Guide to Living Fully in Turbulent Times by Joanna Macy*

Pluto/Uranus

Pluto helps us find our place in the family of things—in the web of life. Pluto supports us in finding our power and using it with wisdom and love. During this transit, we are finding our place in the world and our role as an agent of change and supporter of awakening in this world and beyond.

Read *A Beginner's Guide to Constructing the Universe: Mathematical Archetypes of Nature, Art, and Science by Michael S. Schneider*

Pluto/Neptune

Be available for great visions during this time. Allow a deep transformation to occur that may not make any sense at all. While your inner life roams around in the underworld, this is a perfect and beautiful time for creative projects, spiritual endeavors and quiet, solo retreats. Therapy, mystical practices, meditation, past life journey-work and any vision/dream work are heightened and more powerful during this transit.

Read *Peace is Every Step: The Path of Mindfulness in Everyday Life by Thich Nhat Hanh*

Pluto/Pluto

We are now asked by Pluto to find our power and align our will with a greater evolution that is occurring (perhaps not just on Earth). Evolution is taking place whether we believe it or not. Life changes. As a gift, we have free will—all to use for alignment or to get in the way until we find alignment. During this time we are pushed and confronted with any use of will that is not in alignment with a greater good. We are even confronted when we refuse to use our will to be in alignment. Notice where the confrontations are coming from and do not be afraid to explore, experiment and ask the deep and hard questions of yourself.

Read *Moby Dick by Herman Melville* (Seriously, read it. I just read this out loud to my son and while it is hard to read more than a few chapters at a time, it is a profound look into the soul of humanity.)

Pluto/Ascendant

When Pluto conjuncts the Ascendant or Descendant we are starting a new lifetime within a lifetime. This tends to be the most dramatic transit I witness. The old life must go. This happens once in a lifetime and not in every lifetime.

When Pluto crosses the Ascendant we are moving from lifetimes of focus on a worldly purpose and service to the public into focus on our personal, internal work. The new lifetime that begins with this Pluto transit starts with a new intention for our soul's evolution. We move into doing inner work, more focused on our personal growth and overall path toward enlightenment. Often there is loss during this transit. Something from the old life must go. Sometimes there is a lot of loss. Grief is the work of releasing attachment. This is a grief work time. The easier we let go in the beginning, the sooner the new life begins.

When Pluto crosses the Descendant, we are moving from lifetimes of inner work, lifetimes of playing it small, into having a more significant purpose in the world. Often we have been waiting for this transit in order to really know what the world wants from us. We often need to let go of significant relationships that would hold us back in the new life that is emerging.

Read *I Am That: Talks with Sri Nisargadatta Maharaj* (This is my desert island book.)

Pluto/Midheaven

When Pluto conjuncts the MC, we get powerful messages of what needs to change in our career life. If our job does not allow us to fully express our power, it will likely end. Pluto wants us to fully step into our power. In whatever way we make our life or ourselves too small, Pluto will be a heat-seeking missile for that very issue. If we are here to do greater things, then the small stuff we are attached to will go away. Pluto has two years to do its work and it will not stop 'til it is done. The sooner we let go of the attachment that Pluto has its mind on, the easier the transit goes, the sooner we step into the great new thing that Life has in store for us.

Pluto on the IC often points to a time when we have to let go of the home life or some aspect of home life that is keeping us stuck in old patterns. Sometimes our blood family no longer serves us and we have to let them go. At the beginning of the transit, Pluto will give us a sign for what needs to change. Pay attention. It is often the one thing we are most attached to. Over the course of the transit, it will become clearer that we need to let it go. Remember that Pluto leaves prosperity in its wake.

Read *Autobiography of a Yogi (Self-Realization Fellowship) by Paramahansa Yogananda*

~~~~~~~~~~

Stones for a challenging Pluto transit:

Pluto wants us to let go and experience the bliss of nonattachment. Pluto often supports destruction of things we hold dear so that we can experience this bliss state. **Obsidian** is a powerful stone to bring on the transformation. Be sure you are ready and open for the grief that this stone can unleash. However, if the letting go is painful since it is rubbing up against some fears and attachments, **Smokey Quartz** helps us to let go more gently. **Amethyst** helps us to feel connected to our soul and spirit and **Turquoise** helps us to feel hopeful through seeing the bigger picture. **Spectrolite** (also known as **Labradorite**) is a powerful channeling stone that can lend aid when seeking to understand the underlying meaning during a Pluto transit. **Tourmaline** can provide support us as we negotiate the underworld and release attachment to being a victim.

Pluto through the Houses

Pluto in the 1st House
Pluto transforms our identity, as it moves through the first house. We may feel like we are in a new lifetime and indeed we are. Pluto crossing the Ascendant, which begins Pluto through the 1st house, is one of the most significant life transformations we will experience. We must shed the old persona to make room for the new. Our physical appearance may change. The appearance of our surroundings including people close to us may change. As with all Pluto transits, the sooner we let go of the old, the sooner Pluto offers the new life. Pluto tells us that no one gets out of here alive, so live while you are here.

Pluto in the 2nd House
For this seven-to-twelve year time period, we are finding power through accepting our need to create and be resourceful. Financial challenges are pushing us to be more empowered. If we have a fear of scarcity, Pluto can help us clear these fears. Pluto pushes us to know that abundance is available even in the most difficult situations.

Pluto in the 3rd House
It is time to deepen into our education, to study and learn. We have the chance to explore and be in a body this lifetime. Take this time to travel through new realms. Take an epic road trip without a plan. Find yourself through learning a new trade for no reason other than you are drawn to it.

Pluto in the 4th House
The transformation of this time supports releasing karmic ties with our blood relatives and family. We may search for our true home on this planet. We may long for deeper intimacy. We are finding our truest place on Earth.

Pluto in the 5th House
It is time to find our personal path of creative expression. We are delving into our personal empowerment through how we express ourselves. Uncover a new artistic ability.

Pluto in the 6th House
During this time, we are changing lifetimes of patterns of how we live on this planet. We are changing our lifestyle in a most fundamental way. Focus on healthier eating and sleeping patterns.

Pluto in the 7th House
We are finding our power through relationship. After lifetimes of inner work, this time calls us to be more present in the world, in our work and in following our calling. We want deeper intimacy in our relationships or they will fall by the wayside.

Pluto in the 8th House

We are learning the power of sexual energy as it expresses itself in a human body. We are becoming empowered to do the work that lifetimes have prepared us for.

Pluto in the 9th House

It is time to journey, explore, study and share our wisdom and knowledge. The world needs what we have to share. Pluto pushes us to express it.

Pluto in the 10th House

If we aren't doing what we are here for, Pluto changes everything so that we can. During this time, we must come into right relationship with this world, with our power and with what we have to express and perform on this small and great planet.

Pluto in the 11th House

A time of great recognition can unfold after years of work and empowerment in the world. Allow the gains and recognition of this time to move through you. Practice non-attachment and allow the overflowing abundance of this time.

Pluto in the 12th House

We are releasing lifetimes of work during this time. Our spiritual path becomes an essential and obvious part of our lives. Allow the unknown to be the director of your life.

Appendix A

Stones for the Different Planets

Sign	Ruling Planet	Stones
Aries	Mars	Red coral Carnelian Almondine
Taurus	Venus	Diamond Jade Malachite Lapis Lazuli
Gemini	Mercury	Emerald Peridot Blue Lace Agate Celestite
Cancer	Moon	Moonstone Pearl Opal
Leo	Sun	Ruby Garnet Tiger's Eye
Virgo	Mercury/Chiron	Quartz Blue Lace Agate Celestite Emerald Jade
Libra	Venus	Rose quartz Rhodochrosite Rhodonite

Scorpio	Pluto/Mars	Tourmaline Onyx Carnelian Serpentine
Sagittarius	Jupiter	Turquoise Citrine Topaz
Capricorn	Saturn	Onyx Calcite
Aquarius	Uranus/Saturn	Amber Aquamarine Blue Sapphire
Pisces	Neptune/Jupiter	Amethyst

A note on using stones:

In Vedic astrology, the stones are used specifically as remedies, to powerful effect. Before wearing a ring of a pure gemstone of diamond, ruby, emerald, sapphire, or red coral, I suggest consulting a Vedic astrologer. Of course, many people wear diamond rings on their left ring finger. For many this is a wonderful healing balm. For others, for whom Venus is a challenging planet, the diamond may act in an unsupportive way.

Appendix B

Orbs

Planet	Orb and Timing of a Transit
Moon	7° about half a day
Sun	7° 3 days before and after
Mercury	3° about three days extend to 10° during a retrograde period which lasts for 3 weeks
Venus	3° about five days extend to 10° during a retrograde period which lasts for forty days
Mars	3° about ten days extend to 10° during a retrograde period which lasts about 2 months
Jupiter	3° extend to 5° if Jupiter retrogrades back over the transit point
Nodes	3° extend to include eclipses that trigger the transit
Saturn	3° about a year
Chiron	2° about a year
Uranus	2° about a year and a half
Neptune	2° about two years
Pluto	2° about two years

Appendix C

Geocentric and Heliocentric Perspectives

There are two perspectives that we work with in astrology: geocentric and heliocentric. Geocentric places the Earth in the center of our personal drama, experience and orientation. Heliocentric uses the Sun as the center of the solar system. The geocentric perspective takes into consideration our perspective of the Moon, which is vastly different and inconsequential in the heliocentric perspective. Geocentric is more often used for personal chart interpretation. Heliocentric is often used to observe, track and predict world events.

Tropical and Placidus Zodiacs

There are two zodiac systems. The origin of the word *zodiac* is the same origin as the word *zoo*. The original constellations that encapsulated the ecliptic were named for animals. Over time, constellations have been added that are not animals. We currently have thirteen constellations that the planets revolve through along the orbital plane: Aries, Taurus, Gemini, Cancer, Leo, Virgo, Libra, Scorpio, Ophiuchus, Sagittarius, Capricorn, Aquarius and Pisces. What is easily confused is that the signs of the zodiac used in western astrology are not exactly in alignment with the constellations. In fact they are approximately twenty-four degrees apart from the constellations. This is because the Tropical Zodiac that most western astrologers use begins with the Vernal Equinox. The sky along the ecliptic is divided into twelve equal portions beginning with zero degrees of Aries on the first day of Spring. This aligns the Tropical Zodiac with the seasons, honors our relationship with Earth and has little to do with the actual stars. In western astrology, working with the stars includes tuning into planets as they conjunct a particular star.

In Vedic astrology and in the astrology of the followers of Rudolph Steiner, the Sidereal Zodiac is used. In this zodiac, the constellations as they were divined thousands of years ago align with the zodiac that is used. In Vedic astrology, in addition to the zodiac, there are 27 Nakshatras, often called constellations (adding to the confusion). The Nakshatras are another way of dividing the ecliptic sky. In this case, the planets revolve through twenty-seven sections of sky, each encompassing thirteen degrees and twenty minutes.

Houses Systems

There are many different house systems. This author uses the Placidus House system with success for over twenty years, while being open to Equal, Koch, Porphyry and other systems.

While there is a lot of science in western astrology, there is also a lot of intuition and empathetic perception. An astrologer once told me that we align our intuition with the tool we know. It is a working relationship—knowledge and intuition. For me, I have always worked at both, studying and learning from all the great teachers before me all the while practicing and trusting my inner knowing.

References

Acker, Louis S. and Sakoian, Frances. *The Astrologer's Handbook*. Harper and Row Publishers, New York. 1973.

Addey, John. *Harmonics in Astrology*. Eyebright Books, Wiltshire, UK, 2009.

Bills, Rex E. *The Rulership Book*. AFA, 1971

Hamblin, David. *The Spirit of Numbers: A New Exploration of Harmonic Astrology*. The Wessex Astrologer, Bournemouth, England, 2011.

Hand, Robert. *Planets in Transit: Life Cycles for Living*. Whitford Press, Atglen, PA, 19310.

Houck, Richard. *The Astrology of Death*. Groundswell Press, Gaithersburg, MD, 1994.

Hone, Margaret E. *The Modern Text Book of Astrology*. L.N. Fowler and Co., London. 1951.

Meyers, Eric. *Elements & Evolution: A Spiritual Landscape of Astrology*. Astrology Sight Publishing, Asheville, NC, 2010.

Nauman, Eileen. *Medical Astrology*. Blue Turtle Publishing Cottonwood, AZ. 1993.

Oken, Alan. *Alan Oken's Complete Astrology*. Bantam Books, NY. 1980.

Schulman, Martin. *Karmic Astrology: the Moon's Nodes and Reincarnation, Volume 1*. Samuel Weiser Inc., York Beach, Maine. 1975.

Spiller, Jan. *Astrology for the Soul*. Bantam Books, USA. 1997.

Noel Tyl. *Prediction in Astrology: A Master Volume of Technique and Practice*. Llewellyn Publications, Saint Paul, MN, 1991.

Index

ABOUT THE AUTHOR

Rosie Finn has been a full-time professional astrologer since 1998. She lives in Olympia, Washington, where she sees clients, teaches and lives with her teenage son. Her studies include Western and Vedic astrology, sacred geometry and Sanskrit. For over seventeen years, she offered a popular monthly talk and newsletter called *Plants & Planets*. She is a musician and writer offering lectures, classes, kirtans, and several manuscripts to the world. She is currently working on her upcoming book exploring Pluto in extreme declination.

To find out more about her life and work, go to astrologywithrosiefinn.com.

Made in the USA
Coppell, TX
08 March 2020

16649956R00098